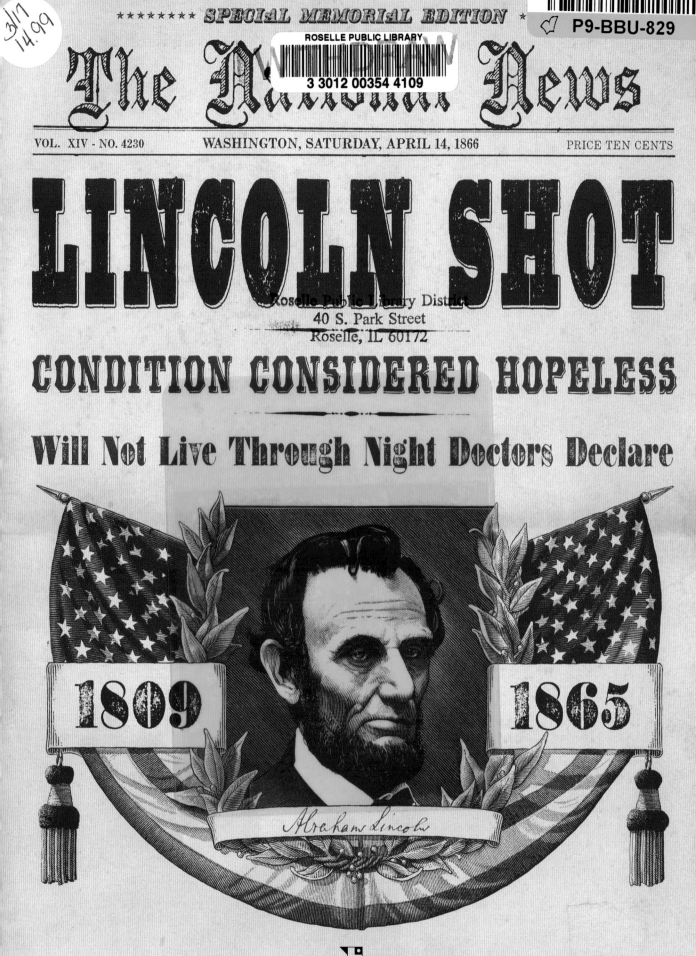

******* SPECIAL MEMORIAL EDITION *******

# The National News

VOL. XIV - NO. 4230    WASHINGTON, SATURDAY, APRIL 14, 1866    PRICE TEN CENTS

# LINCOLN SHOT

## CONDITION CONSIDERED HOPELESS

### Will Not Live Through Night Doctors Declare

1809    1865

*Abraham Lincoln*

SQUARE
FISH
FEIWEL AND FRIENDS
NEW YORK

Where were you on Friday, April 14, 1865, the night President Lincoln was shot?

At this office, we were, within minutes, furiously gathering information and writing articles for the next day's edition.

We have, since that dreadful moment, devoted considerable time to researching, writing, and illustrating Lincoln's exemplary life. Our writers have spent countless hours interviewing those who knew him and crafting his story. Various talented artists have contributed visually in styles that range from simple, but evocative, pencil sketches to the marvelous results of that recent invention, photography.

We begin with a collection of our best articles from the dark days following the assassination. We then tell the story of Abraham Lincoln's life, a compelling presentation of his boyhood, youth, and family; his emergence onto the national political scene; and his presidency and leadership of our country through the Civil War. As we worked, we tried to heed Abraham Lincoln's words of warning:

*"Biographies, as generally written, are not only misleading, but false. The author makes a wonderful hero of his subject. He magnifies his perfections, if he has any, and suppresses his imperfections. History is not history unless it is the truth."*

All of us at *The National News* are proud to present a Special Memorial Edition of our newspaper—a truthful representation of the life and death of our beloved sixteenth president.

# LINCOLN SHOT
## A President's Life Remembered

With you we mourn; with you we remember.

*The Publisher*

# PRESIDENT DIES AT 7:22

## NATION MOURNS FALLEN LEADER

### Evil Deed Creates Sea Of Sorrow Across The Land

The Assassination - Ford's Theater

## JOHN WILKES BOOTH ASSASSIN ESCAPES!

### UNPRECEDENTED MANHUNT

#### All Roads Watched, Arrests Imminent

### MURDERERS POSSIBLY HEADED FOR CANADA

#### Hundreds Of Suspects In Custody—Prisons Overwhelmed

### General Grant Ordered Back To Defend Washington

### CONFEDERATE ARMY RUMORED TO BE HEADED FOR CAPITAL

## PRESIDENT ASSASSINATED

SPECIAL TO THE NATIONAL NEWS
(ORIGINAL ARTICLE APPEARED SAT. MORNING, APRIL 15, 1865)

Abraham Lincoln, the sixteenth president of the United States, was shot by a lone gunman at approximately 10:15 PM last night. He is not expected to live.

The president, Mrs. Lincoln, and their guests, Maj. Rathbone and his fiancée, were watching *Our American Cousin* at Ford's Theater when the heinous crime was committed. Gen. and Mrs. Grant were expected to accompany the president, and it is not known at this time why they were absent.

Sometime earlier, John Wilkes Booth, the

well-known actor whose face was familiar to the employees and players at Ford's, entered the building. At approximately 10:15 PM, while the third act was in progress, Booth handed his calling card to the White House valet and was admitted into the president's box.

The Washington policeman assigned to guard the president had inexplicably left his post. His precise whereabouts during the dastardly attack are not known at this time. There are unconfirmed reports that he had a record of drunkenness, insubordination, and conduct unbecoming an officer.

Booth shot President Lincoln in the back of the head at point-blank range with a .44 caliber, single-shot, Derringer pistol. Most of the 1,700 patrons did not hear the shot because of the laughter elicited by the particular scene being played out on the stage. Even those who did hear something believed it to be part of the plot and not the infinitely more tragic one unfolding in the box above.

After shooting the president, Booth stabbed Maj. Rathbone with a large hunting knife and vaulted over the railing on to the stage 12 feet below. He rose up holding the knife menacingly aloft and, according to some, shouted in Latin *"sic semper tyrannis"*—"thus ever to tyrants." The evil assassin then dashed off the stage and made his way to the alley, where he mounted a getaway horse that was being held for him by an accomplice, and galloped into the night.

The president was unconscious and very near death. A doctor who was in attendance examined the wound and stated that it was fatal. He judged that transporting his gravely wounded patient back to the White House would be unwise. With help from those who had gathered about, he carried the president down the stairs, through the lobby, and onto Tenth Street, where the crowd was cleared by soldiers. One of the residents of a boardinghouse facing the theater cried out, "Bring him in here."

At 11:00 PM Secy. of War Edwin Stanton arrived and took complete charge of the situation. The secretary was already aware that simultaneously with the attack on the president, Secy. of State William Seward had been assailed in his home and seriously injured by a madman who wounded several members of the household in a bloody rampage. The assailant was finally beaten off and fled. His identity and whereabouts are unknown at this time.

Secy. Stanton contacted Gen. Grant:

War Department, Washington
April 14 midnight (sent 12:20 PM)

To Lieut. Gen. US GRANT
On the night train to Burlington

The President was assassinated at Ford's Theater at 10:30 tonight & cannot live. The wound is a Pistol shot through the head. Secretary Seward & his son Frederick, were also assassinated at their residences & are in dangerous condition. The Secretary of War desires that you return to Washington immediately. Please answer on receipt of this.

The president never regained consciousness, was paralyzed, had a very weak pulse, and had great difficulty breathing. By 6:00 AM, his condition had worsened, and by 7:22 AM, he was dead.

# THE PRESIDENT'S DAY

EXCLUSIVE REPORT
(ORIGINAL ARTICLE APPEARED SUN. EVENING, APRIL 16, 1865)

On Friday morning, April 14, 1865, the president awoke at 7:00 AM, lit a fire, worked on some papers, and read the newspaper. Mrs. Lincoln and their son Robert joined him in the family dining room for breakfast. Robert and his father talked over his plans to resume his law studies.

At 11:00 AM, the president met with the Cabinet, including Gen. Grant. Many Cabinet members noted the neat appearance the usually quite disheveled president made and his generally relaxed demeanor. They attributed these changes to the terrible burden of the war being lifted at long last from his shoulders.

After the meeting, Gen. Grant informed the president that he and Mrs. Grant were going to visit their children in New Jersey and would not, as previously agreed, be able to accompany him and Mrs. Lincoln to the theater. It is well known that Mrs. Grant disliked Mrs. Lincoln; this was possibly an additional reason for their decision not to go to the theater.

Having no time for lunch, the president made do with an apple and, as usual, visited the telegraph office in the War Department, issued pardons, and met with people. He also gave some visitors lemons from the tree he recently received as a gift.

At 3:00 PM, he and Mary went for a carriage ride, as was their custom. Mary was pleased to see how cheerful her husband was. He said that: *"We must be more cheerful in the future; between the war and the loss of our darling Willie, we have been very miserable."*

He talked about his plans for the future, which included traveling to California and Europe. The president was looking forward to returning to his law practice in Springfield, Illinois, at the end of his term.

They returned to the White House at 5:00 PM, where the president had still more meetings and paperwork to confront.

At 6:00 PM, he had dinner with the family. Mary had one of her headaches and suggested that they stay home. This appealed to her husband, who was tired to the bone. But he thought he had a better chance at getting some peace and quiet at the theater than he would at the always tumultuous White House. He felt obliged to go since his appearance had been announced already in the newspaper and he didn't want to disappoint people.

The president and Mrs. Lincoln entered their carriage at a little after 8:00 PM, picked up Maj. Rathbone and Miss Harris, and arrived at Ford's Theater at 8:30 PM.

The play, which had already begun, was halted as President Lincoln was greeted with a standing ovation while the orchestra played "Hail to the Chief." He smiled, acknowledged the warm greeting, and settled into the rocking chair that had been put there for him.

Behind that rocking chair, in the shadows, the assassin lurked.

# PROFILE OF AN ASSASSIN

(ORIGINAL ARTICLE APPEARED SAT. MORNING, APRIL 22, 1865)

John Wilkes Booth was born in 1838, not far from Baltimore, Maryland. He was the next to the youngest of ten children but was, from the very first, his mother's favorite. His father, a mentally unstable alcoholic, was a famous actor, as was John's older brother. When he was 17, Booth made his acting debut and became known for his athletic style, which featured great leaps and flamboyant sword fights.

Exotically handsome with curly black hair, an attractive mustache, and penetrating hazel eyes, Booth was as popular with the ladies as he was with audiences. Vain, stylish, moody, and undisciplined, Booth, like his father, was known to drink more than his share.

It appears that Booth, who was an outspoken advocate of slavery from an early age, had been plotting to kidnap the president of the United States since October 1864. The charismatic and persuasive actor was able to recruit a number of willing accomplices. Operating out of a Washington hotel, Booth funded the extensive operation with his considerable acting income.

Booth intended to take the president forcibly to Richmond, where he would be exchanged for captured Confederate soldiers being held in Northern prisons. Booth speculated that this ungodly act might even throw the entire government into chaos and,

*John Wilkes Booth*

somehow, lead to Southern independence.

On March 4, 1865, Booth was present during Lincoln's second inauguration ceremony. He saw how exposed the president could be at times.

Two weeks later, he and the others attempted to kidnap President Lincoln at gunpoint, but their plans went awry when the president's itinerary changed and Lincoln was not where Booth thought he would be. There is also evidence that Booth planned to kidnap Lincoln from Ford's Theater by tying him with a rope and lowering him to the stage.

In early April, when Union troops marched into the Confederate capital and, days later, the main rebel army surrendered, Booth realized that kidnapping would serve no useful purpose. Angered at the South's defeat and wanting, as always, to make a name for himself in the history books, Booth began to consider killing, rather than kidnapping, the president.

On April 11, President Lincoln, standing in the window of the White House balcony, delivered a carefully considered speech about allowing blacks to vote. Booth, in the crowd on the lawn below, was enraged by this and vowed it would be the last speech the president would make.

Three days later, at noon on Friday, April

SURRAT.     BOOTH.     HAROLD.

# War Department, Washington, April 20, 1865,

# $100,000 REWARD!

# THE MURDERER

## Of our late beloved President, Abraham Lincoln,

# IS STILL AT LARGE.

# $50,000 REWARD

Will be paid by this Department for his apprehension, in addition to any reward offered by Municipal Authorities or State Executives.

# $25,000 REWARD

Will be paid for the apprehension of JOHN H. SURRATT, one of Booth's Accomplices.

# $25,000 REWARD

Will be paid for the apprehension of David C. Harold, another of Booth's accomplices.

LIBERAL REWARDS will be paid for any information that shall conduce to the arrest of either of the above-named criminals, or their accomplices.

All persons harboring or secreting the said persons, or either of them, or aiding or assisting their concealment or escape, will be treated as accomplices in the murder of the President and the attempted assassination of the Secretary of State, and shall be subject to trial before a Military Commission and the punishment of DEATH.

Let the stain of innocent blood be removed from the land by the arrest and punishment of the murderers.

All good citizens are exhorted to aid public justice on this occasion. Every man should consider his own conscience charged with this solemn duty, and rest neither night nor day until it be accomplished.

### EDWIN M. STANTON, Secretary of War.

DESCRIPTIONS.—BOOTH is Five Feet 7 or 8 inches high, slender build, high forehead, black hair, black eyes, and wears a heavy black moustache.

JOHN H. SURRAT is about 5 feet, 9 inches. Hair rather thin and dark; eyes rather light; no beard. Would weigh 145 or 150 pounds. Complexion rather pale and clear, with color in his cheeks. Wore light clothes of fine quality. Shoulders square; cheek bones rather prominent; chin narrow; ears projecting at the top; forehead rather low and square, but broad. Parts his hair on the right side; neck rather long. His lips are firmly set. A slim man.

DAVID C. HAROLD is five feet six inches high, hair dark, eyes dark, eyebrows rather heavy, full face, nose short, hand short and fleshy, feet small, instep high, round bodied, naturally quick and active, slightly closes his eyes when looking at a person.

NOTICE.—In addition to the above, State and other authorities have offered rewards amounting to almost one hundred thousand dollars, making an aggregate of about TWO HUNDRED THOUSAND DOLLARS.

14, Booth went to Ford's Theater to pick up his mail and learned that the Lincolns were coming to the play that evening. He decided to assassinate the president that very night.

Moving frantically and working furiously all afternoon, Booth met with his accomplices and implemented his, by now, expanded plan. He now planned to orchestrate the murder of the vice president and the secretary of state. Booth hoped to decapitate the government of the United States.

By 8:30 PM, when the president's carriage pulled up to the front doors of Ford's Theater, all the pieces of his nefarious plan were in place.

MARY SURRATT

LEWIS POWELL

DAVID HEROLD

GEORGE ATZERODT

# ASSASSINS APPREHENDED

## SECY. SEWARD'S ASSAILANT AND TWO OTHERS ARRESTED

## Vicious Madman Identified

## Blood Found on Clothes

## FURTHER ARRESTS HOURS AWAY

## BOOTH'S CAPTURE ASSURED BY AUTHORITIES

### Conflicting Reports Concerning Escape Route

# SUSPECTS ARRESTED

(ORIGINAL ARTICLE APPEARED SAT. EVENING, APRIL 22, 1865)

Three of John Wilkes Booth's known conspirators have been arrested by the authorities, and government sources indicate that more arrests are certain to follow. Hundreds of suspects are being questioned concerning their involvement in what is apparently a vast, intricate, and well-financed Confederate conspiracy.

Details of the arrests are as follows.

Mary Surratt, 41, widow, mother of known Confederate courier John Surratt, and associate of John Wilkes Booth. Mrs. Surratt owned a Maryland tavern, which was identified as a center of Confederate secret service activity. In 1864, she moved to Washington and opened a boardinghouse on H Street, which also served as a clandestine Confederate communications center.

Mrs. Surratt was arrested within hours of the infernal act at her H Street boardinghouse.

Lewis Powell, 21, Alabama-born rebel soldier taken prisoner at Gettysburg and released. Two brothers killed in war and one who lost his leg. Large, strong, silent, and violent, he is known to have kept the skull of a Union soldier as an ashtray.

Powell has been identified beyond any doubt as the man who attacked and nearly killed Secy. of State Seward. He is believed to have been abandoned by his partner, 22-year-old David Herold, who is still at large. Herold was to have guided Powell through the streets of the city and into Maryland. However, when he heard the bloodcurdling screams coming from the Seward house, he, apparently, ran for his life, leaving Powell lost in the unfamiliar Washington streets.

Powell was arrested by soldiers stationed at Surratt's boardinghouse, where he unexpectedly appeared.

George Atzerodt, 29, alcoholic, German immigrant, and carriage painter. Atzerodt was arrested on April 20 at his cousin's house in Maryland. Reportedly, he balked at his assigned task of murdering Vice President Andrew Johnson and wandered the streets alone that night. He has given the authorities valuable information about the inner workings of the conspiracy.

# OUR MARTYRED PRESIDENT

## Tragedy of the Century

### Funeral Held in East Room of White House

### Lincoln Lies in State Awaiting Trip Back to Springfield for Burial

### Funeral Train to Take Same Route as Four Years Earlier

### "Now he belongs to the ages"

# BOOTH CAPTURED AND KILLED

### Unprecedented Twelve Day Manhunt in Maryland and Virginia

### Discovered in Tobacco Barn Herold Surrenders

### Booth refuses to be taken alive Barn set on fire Shot in neck and dies hours later

# BOOTH
## CAPTURED & KILLED

(ORIGINAL ARTICLE APPEARED APRIL 26, 1865 IN A NATIONAL NEWS ONE-PAGE EXTRA)

After committing his cowardly and dastardly deed, John Wilkes Booth raced his getaway horse down the alley behind Ford's Theater, into the nighttime streets of Washington, and past unsuspecting soldiers. He was headed for the Navy Yard Bridge, the quickest route across the Potomac into southern Maryland and the safety of the South.

Booth reached the bridge at 10:45 PM on April 14 and was detained, as required, by the sentry who asked his name, residence, and destination. The bold killer, calling on his well-known acting abilities, calmly and candidly answered all questions put to him.

The sentry warned that he would not be permitted to return and then let the assassin of the president of the United States escape.

A few minutes later, David Herold, who had left Powell at the Seward house, arrived and was stopped by the same sentry and also allowed to pass.

Booth and Herold, traveling faster than the news of their foul deed, were able to stay ahead of the government dragnet that had already begun to descend over them.

Herold caught up with his leader and they headed, as planned, eight miles south, to the Surratt tavern. Encountering no one on the road at that hour, they arrived at midnight and picked up rifles, ammunition, and field glasses—all of which Booth had ordered Mary Surratt to have waiting for them. They also took some whiskey for the pain in Booth's leg, which he apparently had broken while leaping from the president's box to the stage at Ford's Theater.

Booth and Herold immediately headed for the house of Dr. Mudd, another one of the vast network of rebel accomplices Booth had put in place over the past year. Arriving four hours later, the good doctor put a splint on Booth's leg so he could hobble around and fashioned crude crutches to further aid the fugitive's mobility.

Leaving Dr. Mudd, the assassin and his underling continued to flee. Along the way, they were helped by more rebel soldiers, agents, and Southern sympathizers who provided them with food, clothing, shelter, transportation, and places to hide from the constantly closing federal forces.

By April 25, Booth had been spotted. By 2:00 AM the next day, the soldiers of the sixteenth New York Cavalry had tracked him down to a Virginia farm 60 miles south of Washington, where he and Herold were hiding in a tobacco barn.

The soldiers descended on the farm and surrounded the barn. Herold surrendered but Booth refused. He challenged the soldiers to step back from the barn so he could emerge and engage them in a fair fight. Wanting to capture him alive, the soldiers set fire to the barn, hoping to smoke Booth out.

Booth's movements could be seen through the openings in the barn walls. He retreated to the center of the barn away from the rapidly encroaching flames. Wary soldiers watched as he attempted to support himself on one of Dr. Mudd's crutches while bracing and readying his rifle against his hip.

Fearing that he was about to start firing at them, one of the soldiers, acting on his own and hoping only to wound the dangerous assassin, shot him. Booth, mortally wounded, was taken from the barn and died in agony a few hours later.

# EXTRAORDINARY SECURITY MEASURES FOR TRAGIC TRIAL

## ASSASSINS TO WEAR CANVAS HOODS

## COMPLETE SECLUSION

### NO INFORMATION AND COMMUNICATION

### MUST TAKE FOOD THROUGH HOLES

## Prisoners Manacled Hand and Foot During Trial

### Mrs. Surratt Wears Veil to hide face from Sketch Artists
### Lifts it only when Being Identified by Witnesses

Powell Bangs Head Against Wall in Suicide Attempt
Hands Manacled
Special Padded Hood Constructed

# EXECUTION

(ORIGINAL ARTICLE APPEARED ON JULY 7, 1865)

On the morning of July 7, 1865, mounted soldiers waited at intervals between the White House and the prison, anticipating a presidential pardon for Mary Surratt. She would be the first woman executed by the federal government. Mrs. Surratt's daughter, Anna, went to the White House seeking mercy for her mother. President Johnson refused to see her.

Outside the prison gates, vendors sold lemonade to the gathering crowd. Inside, soldiers, government officials, press, and spectators who were able to get one of the precious tickets waited. Still others watched from the windows of the penitentiary and the roof of a building on the grounds.

The cells the condemned had been transferred to faced the prison yard, and the prisoners could hear the gallows being hastily constructed during the night. In the morning, they could also hear the traps being tested with 300-pound weights.

At noon, friends, family, and loved ones of the doomed assassins were asked to leave so that the four could prepare for their executions.

A little after 1:00 PM, Mary Surratt emerged followed by Lewis Powell, George Atzerodt, and David Herold, their chains clanking. They were led across the courtyard and past their ammunition crate coffins and recently dug graves. Mrs. Surratt was wearing a bonnet and a black veil to hide her face. She had trouble walking and had to be supported. Her daughter's screams were audible throughout the prison and across the yard.

They were taken up the 13 steps to the top of the scaffold. Mrs. Surratt was provided with a small chair and an umbrella to shield her from the excessive (100-degree) summer sun. Their arms and legs were bound by white cloth so that they would not flail. White hoods were placed over their heads, Mrs. Surratt's veil and bonnet having been removed first. She was having difficulty standing and asked those around her to not allow her to fall.

The ropes were placed around their necks; the executioner gave the signal; the soldiers knocked out the posts that were holding up the floor; and the four fell to their deaths.

# NINE-MAN MILITARY TRIBUNAL REACHES VERDICT

## SEVEN-WEEK TRIAL OVER

## Assassins Doomed

# DEATH BY HANGING

## Surratt, Powell, Atzerodt, Herold to Die Simultaneously

### Death Warrants Delivered and Read to Condemned

### Execution within Twenty-four Hours

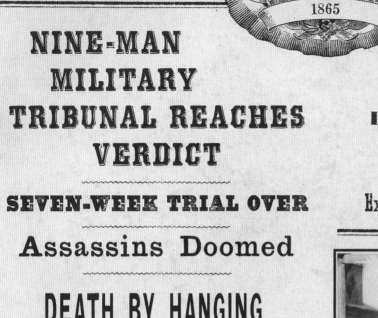

*The assassins hang at Old Arsenal Penitentiary, Washington, D.C.*

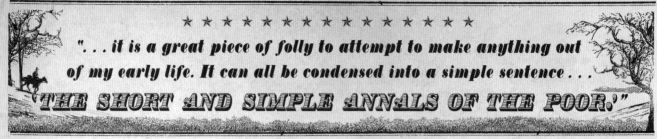

★ ★ ★ ★ ★ ★ ★ ★ ★ ★ ★ ★ ★ ★ ★

*". . . it is a great piece of folly to attempt to make anything out of my early life. It can all be condensed into a simple sentence . . .*

## "THE SHORT AND SIMPLE ANNALS OF THE POOR."

# BOYHOOD
## (1809-1829)

### KENTUCKY • INDIANA • FAMILY
### STEPMOTHER • SCHOOLING

Abraham Lincoln was born during the early morning hours of Sunday, February 12, 1809, in a small, one-room cabin that his father had built. It had a hard-packed dirt floor, no glass in the windows, and a large fireplace.

Like many homes in the Kentucky wilderness, it was a simple but sturdy dwelling.

Abraham's father, Thomas, was a slow-moving, plain-speaking farmer and carpenter. Thomas could read a little and sign his name, though with difficulty. Mostly, he liked to tell humorous stories—a characteristic he passed on to his son along with his physical strength.

Nancy, his mother, although illiterate, was considered intelligent. Abraham probably inherited his uncommon intellectual capabilities and melancholy nature from her. A sense of sadness seemed to envelope Nancy Lincoln, as it would her son.

In 1806, Nancy Hanks had married Thomas, and Sarah, their first child, was born within a year. A third child was born a few years after Abraham, but lived only days.

When Abraham was seven, Thomas

Lincoln, a restless man, moved his family to Indiana, where he believed the farmland was more properly governed by federal law.

They traveled on horseback, flatboat, and wagon. The 100-mile journey took two weeks.

Indiana was a wild and remote land of vast forests; a wide variety of trees grew tall and strong. Some oaks measured 20 feet or more in circumference. The woods were filled with raccoons, squirrels, partridges, and wildcats. At night, bears and panthers could be heard ominously in the not-too-far distance.

In Indiana, the underbrush was so dense that they had to hack their way to the parcel Thomas Lincoln had selected weeks earlier. Upon arrival, they set about the hard work of felling trees and clearing the land. Abraham fetched the water from the spring that was more than a mile away—an inexplicable, fundamental error when choosing a site.

They ate the turkey, deer, and other wild game that Thomas hunted, and the children wore the animal skins or the clothes from cloth their mother spun.

They barely survived the first year.

Eventually, Thomas built another, larger log cabin. This one was tall enough for a loft, which was where Abraham slept after climbing up the pegs that were driven into the wall.

When Abraham was nine, his mother became ill from "milk sickness," which came from the milk of cows that had eaten something poisonous. There was no known cure. A week later, after telling Abraham and Sarah to be good to their father and each other, 34-year-old Nancy Lincoln was buried in a coffin her husband built.

Thomas Lincoln, faced with two young children to care for and the harsh reality of frontier life in the early 1800s, returned to Kentucky and sought out Sarah Bush Johnston. He had courted her, unsuccessfully, before marrying Nancy. She was now widowed with three children, ages 5, 8, and 12. He presented his case matter-of-factly: They both needed spouses; they had known each other since they were young; and there was no time to waste.

Sarah was concerned about leaving without paying her debts, but Thomas took the list, paid everyone that night, and the next morning, they were married.

Along with her three children and their cat, Thomas's new wife accompanied him back to Indiana, where they surprised Abraham and his sister with their new stepfamily. The wagon carried all of Sarah's worldly possessions: a handsome bureau; a table and chairs; pots, pans and utensils; proper bedding; and a spinning wheel. To the Lincoln children, it looked like a mountain of gold.

Young Abraham

Sarah Bush Johnston, now Lincoln, wasted no time. She informed her new husband that a proper floor was to be put down and doors and windows hung, that the cracks in between the logs had to be filled, and the corn-husk mats they slept on replaced with the feather beds she had brought.

Seeing the filthy, ragged, undernourished condition of the children, she introduced the concept of cleanliness, mended their clothes and gave them some of her children's, and took over the cooking chores from young Sarah.

Gentle and caring, she created a warm family feeling from the moment she arrived in the now-crowded cabin, where everyone was treated equally—almost.

The truth was that Abraham, who proved to be obedient, willing, and appreciative, quickly became her favorite.

She wanted him to go to school more regularly. He had gone with his older sister when she walked two miles to the "*blab school*" (so called because the students recited their lessons simultaneously out loud, the loudness being a sign of their diligence).

He could "*spell down*" the whole class, meaning he won the spelling bees. Once, a strict teacher threatened to keep the entire class all day and all night until someone spelled "*defied*" correctly. When a female classmate faltered after the "*f*," Abraham, as eager to be helpful as he was to go home, pointed slyly to his eye. Class dismissed.

But he went to school "*by littles*," as he put it, only when he wasn't helping his father. His father cared nothing for reading and less for learning. He wanted Abraham to help him with the backbreaking chores that always needed doing on a frontier farm: chopping wood, filling the wood box, cleaning the ashes out of the fireplace, clearing and plowing the fields, splitting rails, erecting fences and checking them, and thrashing wheat and hauling it to the gristmill. The last nearly proved fatal.

One day, Abraham took a load of corn to be ground into meal. In a hurry to get back before dark, he whipped the horse, which returned the favor by kicking him in the forehead and knocking him unconscious for hours— "*apparently killed for a time*"—as Lincoln phrased it.

Abraham was legally obligated to turn over all of his earnings to his father until he was 21. Thomas hired him out to other farmers and collected the pay. Abraham exhibited the same lazy attitudes toward these jobs as he did toward his own chores. His father was well aware that he wasn't lazy when it came to things that interested him, like reading and learning.

Abraham had been reading since he discovered books: "***The things I want to know are in books; my best friend is the man who'll git me a book I ain't read.***"

He carried one with him everywhere, especially when doing his chores. Too often, Thomas Lincoln would find his son lying under a tree, book in hand, the plow and the horse "resting."

Abraham read to gain knowledge, to become wise in the ways of the world. He read *Aesop's Fables, Robinson Crusoe, The Pilgrim's Progress*, the works of Shakespeare, U.S. history, and biographies of Washington and Franklin.

Around the house, he did his numbers with charcoal on boards or wooden shovels— anything he could find because paper was scarce. What paper he was able to get he fashioned into a copybook in which he wrote down things he considered worthwhile. His penmanship was so good the neighbors asked him to write letters for them.

Sometimes he composed poems:

*Abraham Lincoln*
*his pad and pen*
*he will be good but*
*god knows when.*


*Abraham Lincoln is my nam[e]*
*And with my pen I wrote the same*
*I wrote in both haste and speed*
*and left it here for fools to read*


Abraham got along well with his new stepbrothers and sisters and his 19-year-old cousin, Dennis Hanks. Dennis had come to live with them the year Abraham's mother died, when Dennis's parents also succumbed to the milk sickness.

They swam, hiked, and climbed trees, but didn't fish or hunt as Abraham didn't care much for killing animals. Abraham refused to join with some of the local boys when they put hot coals on turtles so that the animals would be forced to come out of their shells, and he wasn't shy about telling the other boys how much he disapproved.

———————

When he was 17, his sister married and moved several miles away. When she died giving birth about a year and a half later, he blamed his brother-in-law (whom he had never liked) for failing to send for the doctor.

When told of her death, Lincoln sat down, buried his face in his hands, and sobbed.

*"In this sad world of ours, sorrow comes to all; and, to the young, it come with bitterest agony because it takes them unawares. . . . I have had experience enough to know what I say."*

*A page from Abraham's sum books*

# YOUTH
## (1830-1835)

## ILLINOIS · WORK · NEW SALEM MILITIA · POLITICS

In March 1830, Thomas Lincoln, alarmed by reports of another outbreak of milk sickness and enticed by the prospect of more fertile land, sold his farm and moved his family to Illinois.

While fording a swollen stream in their ox-drawn wagon, Abraham's dog got left behind. Fearful of the ice chunks swirling in the frigid water below, he remained on the bank, barking frantically. Thomas decided there was no choice—they would have to continue on without him. His son disagreed.

*"Pulling off shoes and socks I waded across the stream and triumphantly returned with the shivering animal under my arm. His frantic leaps of joy and other evidence of a dog's gratitude amply repaid me for the exposure I had undergone."*

They settled near New Salem (pop. 100), a growing town with a justice of the peace, a blacksmith, two saloons, two doctors, a hatmaker, a sawmill, a general store, and a ferry that operated across the river.

Abraham worked a variety of jobs, including hiring out with a crew that was taking cargo down to New Orleans and back—a 3-month, 1,200-mile journey. This gave him a much-needed break from his father, who now added Abraham's lack of religion to his other complaints.

Abraham refused to join the Baptist church his father belonged to, even after his much-loved stepmother became a member. Abraham believed there was a higher power, but didn't want to follow any particular religion. He preferred to have his own thoughts about the existence of the Deity.

He built a flatboat that he used to take the produce from the family farm down the river to sell at market. Standing on the landing one day, two men asked him if he and his boat were available to take them and their luggage out to the steamboat midriver. Abraham took them and they each rewarded him with a silver half-dollar, quite a bit of money at the time, especially for a young man.

*"You may think it was a very little thing, but it was a most important incident in my life. I could scarcely believe that I, a poor boy, had earned a dollar in less than a day. The world seemed wider and fairer to me. I was a more hopeful and confident being from that time."*

His favorite job was in New Salem, where he worked as a clerk in one of the grocery stores. There he could listen to the locals and add his own humorous stories to the mix. He would sit out front and read newspapers and letters to the townspeople, some who were unable to read. He even had a room of his own in the back where he slept.

The store owner liked him and was impressed with the strength of his muscular, 6'4" 180-pound clerk. All those years of hard work had paid off. More than good with an ax, he could sink the blade deep into the trunk of a tree. If he was of a mind to show off, he could hold the ax by the end of the handle at arm's length.

The store owner started telling people that his new clerk could beat anyone at wrestling, including the aptly named Jack Armstrong, reigning local champion. Abraham, trapped and not wanting to appear afraid (a bad move on the frontier), agreed to the fight. Money, knives, whiskey, and various other items were bet on the much-anticipated and well-attended match.

Some say Armstrong won fair and square, others Lincoln. Some say that Armstrong tricked Lincoln, or that his friends ganged up on him, and Lincoln courageously offered to take them on, one at a time. One thing is certain, Abraham emerged with his reputation enhanced, and eventually, he and Armstrong became friends. People in New Salem liked Abraham because he always acted naturally and was never false. They admired his intelligence and enjoyed his unique sense of humor and lively conversation. They were aware of his growing reputation for justice and fair play.

He was becoming popular and gaining self-confidence as a result.

---

In April 1832, Lincoln enlisted in the state militia being formed to fight the Indians. The pay was good, it promised to be exciting, and everyone was doing it. Besides, military experience might be good for someone who was considering politics as a career. Much to his surprise, he was elected captain and Jack Armstrong was his first sergeant.

One day, his men were marching 20 abreast, heading for a fence with a gate in the middle. Captain Lincoln, unfamiliar as he was with such military technicalities as proper drilling commands, was unable to order his men to march sideways so that they might go through the gate two by two. Coolly considering his options, he commanded his men to halt and break ranks. He dismissed them and ordered them to reform in two minutes on the other side of the gate.

Sometime after this, a weary, hungry, elderly Black Hawk Indian happened into their camp, bearing a letter of safe conduct from a general citing his service to white people. Lincoln's men believed he was a spy, and even if he wasn't,

Abraham Lincoln and Jack Armstrong fight — New Salem, Illinois

wanted to kill him. Lincoln refused and forced his men to back down.

Although he reenlisted twice, he saw no action. Later, he would say his bloodiest encounter was with the mosquitoes. His experience successfully commanding a company of men not much inclined to take orders would serve him well in the future.

———————————

Lincoln continued what was becoming a rigorous self-education program. *"He studied with nobody"* was how he put it. A book was his constant companion and he sought out anyone who might have something to teach, such as the blacksmith who knew a little poetry and a lot of Shakespeare.

He spent hours perfecting his grammar and improving his public speaking and writing skills. He began to hang around the courthouse, listening intensely as lawyers cross-examined witnesses and delivered impassioned summations. He noted how they practiced the art of convincing juries and thought it was something he just might like to try himself. He thought he might be good at it.

The idea of becoming a lawyer, and perhaps even, someday, entering politics, appealed to him. Even with his lack of formal schooling—he had been in school only a total of maybe one year—it was possible, especially in the newly expanding western United States.

Lincoln studied the Declaration of Independence and the Constitution and borrowed books and read up on Illinois law. He read some cases twice, rewriting the arguments in his own words so that he truly knew them. Impressed by his familiarity with state law, his friends and neighbors called upon him to draw up deeds, contracts, mortgages, and other legal papers.

At meetings of the debating club he joined, his hands-in-the-pocket style and voice that was just a little too high didn't win anyone over, but the persuasive power of his argument and the forceful nature of his reasoning did.

When he gave his first political speech, which was serious and substantive, he surprised his friends who were expecting some more funny stories. He was clearly a young man with a future. His friends urged him to consider entering politics, which was precisely what ambitious Abraham had in mind. New Salem needed someone to represent them in the state legislature, and Lincoln agreed to run.

The aspiring politician presented his philosophy with what would become his characteristic candor, humility, and humor:

*"Fellow Citizens, I presume you all know who I am. I am humble Abraham Lincoln. I have been solicited by many friends to be a candidate for the Legislature. My politics are short and sweet, like the old woman's dance.*

*"If elected I shall be thankful; if not, it will be all the same.*

*". . . If the good people in their wisdom shall see fit to keep me in the background, I have been too familiar with disappointments to be very much chagrined."*

Although he lost, in the New Salem precinct he got 277 of the 300 votes.

———————————

In an ill-advised move, he opened his own general store. His partner turned out to be someone who preferred drinking to selling, while Abraham preferred talking politics to talking inventory. It wasn't long before the store, in Lincoln's words, *"winked out."*

With a little help from his friends, he was appointed postmaster. The post office was

1830-1835

located in the general store, which gave Abraham the opportunity to keep tabs on the current political discussions he was becoming increasingly interested in. The mail arrived once a week, first by post rider, and later, by stagecoach. There were no stamps or envelopes, so letters arrived as folded sheets of paper that were closed with a wax seal.

The postmaster calculated the mailing cost, which was paid by the recipient, by the number of pages and, after looking at the postmark, the distance traveled. Then he marked the final tabulation on the upper right-hand corner.

Lincoln made sure he read all the newspapers that came in first though. Then he put the mail in his hat (a lifelong place for important documents) and made his appointed rounds. He often left the doors of the store unlocked so the townspeople could come and go as they pleased. The postmaster job did not pay enough, but fortunately the overworked town surveyor needed help.

Abraham borrowed some books, a compass and chain, and taught himself how to survey. He surveyed roads, schools, and farms, marking boundaries by blazing trees and piling up brush in the corners. He became known for the accuracy of his surveys. There is one story, however, about a parcel that he surveyed incorrectly, but on purpose. The correct boundaries, it seemed, would have put the widow and family of a man who had served under him in the militia out on the street.

In August 1834, two years after his defeat, Lincoln, age 25, ran again and won. He arrived in Vandalia, the state capital, wearing a new suit he bought with money he borrowed from a friend, and took a room in a tavern.

When the Illinois House of Representatives wasn't in session, he would return to New Salem, deliver the mail, and continue to survey property to supplement his income. John Stuart, a lawyer who Lincoln met while in the militia (and who had lent him the law books), encouraged him to intensify his law studies. He studied incessantly, so incessantly that his friends became alarmed about his health; he was looking even paler and thinner than usual.

His friends were also concerned about his mental state. He had always been eccentric: moody and melancholy, someone who clearly felt and thought more seriously about things than most people. His jokes and funny stories were attempts to counterbalance his somber nature. He was, some felt, sensitive to a fault. You could see it in his light-green eyes, so light they looked gray and eerie.

Some suspected that it wasn't just his relentless study habits, but personal problems that were weighing him down—problems that the secretive Abraham kept to himself.

The situation became so serious that Lincoln agreed to go to the secluded home of an older couple who had befriended him. There he was watched over, cared for, and fed hot biscuits covered in honey.

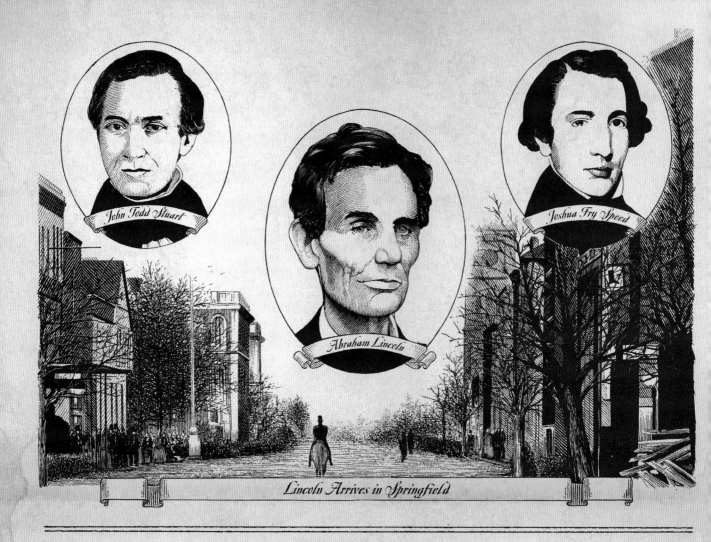

*Lincoln Arrives in Springfield*

# POLITICIAN

## (1836-1853)

### SPRINGFIELD · ROMANCE
### MARRIAGE · FATHERHOOD
### LAW OFFICE · CONGRESSMAN
### WASHINGTON · EDDIE

In September 1836, Abraham Lincoln was admitted to the bar, and the following April, he moved to Springfield, Illinois, to join John Stuart's law practice.

Springfield (pop. 1,500), 16 miles away from New Salem, was even larger than Vandalia. There were 19 dry goods stores, 18 doctors, 11 lawyers, 4 drugstores, 4 hotels, and a bookstore. You could buy anything from Cuban cigars to sperm whale oil. The streets were laid out in a grid and were numbered and named (the east-west ones after presidents). No one went barefoot and most wore shoes and boots instead of moccasins. The women wore silk and lace and rode around in carriages that looked as fine as they did. It was quite something for the rural farm boy.

A half block away from Lincoln's new office was Joshua Speed's general store, which sold groceries, hardware, books, medicine, bedclothes, mattresses, and more. Speed knew who Lincoln was—his budding reputation having preceded him. Recognizing Lincoln's woeful financial state, Speed offered to let Lincoln share his room over the store, rent free. Lincoln picked up his saddlebags, which contained a few law books and fewer clothes, and said, *"Well, Speed, I am moved"* (perhaps meaning both physically and emotionally). He and Lincoln hit it off and became lifelong friends.

Stuart, two years older and already a highly respected lawyer and prominent politician, became Lincoln's mentor. He believed his new partner possessed an exceptional legal mind and had real political potential. Stuart's law firm was one of the state's largest and most prestigious. Because Stuart was busy conducting his campaign for the U.S. Congress, Lincoln took on the majority of their cases.

He lost one murder case when his client was convicted of killing someone in a drunken brawl and was subsequently hanged, and won one defending a politician who had killed another politician in a dispute over an elective office. Lincoln's summation to the jury was considered at least partially responsible for his client's acquittal.

As a legislator, Lincoln continued the political apprenticeship he had begun in Vandalia. He learned what was required to successfully guide a bill through the intricate and treacherous legislative maze. He studied the art of political persuasion and compromise, coming to see that substance wasn't nearly as important as influence and that righteousness had to be tempered with reality. He began to form the alliances he would need in the future.

Lincoln spoke out on and debated a variety of topics: *"internal improvements,"* meaning the expansion of the network of canals, roads, and railroads that were spreading across the American landscape; immigration—both from Europe and the eastern states, westward; and the effects of the tripling of the population.

The young legislator was proving to be an eloquent and effective speaker and was reelected three times, becoming his party's state leader.

And he had an edge. Lincoln could resort to tactics that could easily be considered unseemly and on occasion would display his temper, even to the point of being physically confrontational. Speaking to a crowd once, he saw a colleague being attacked and strode off the stage platform and down into the crowd, where he took on the assailant. He had been known to threaten unruly crowds.

And there were times, despite his own speeches to the contrary, when he seemed to believe that acting outside the law was the only way to right a wrong.

Near their law office was a man who drank too much and consistently hit his wife. Lincoln warned the man numerous times that if he didn't stop he would beat him. When the man didn't stop, Lincoln and his friends grabbed him, tore off his shirt, tied him to a post, and got his wife to administer a whipping. There were no future problems with the man.

Abraham Lincoln was making progress: becoming independent from his father; improving his financial situation; and carving out a career and possible future in politics. But when it came to romance, the sure-footed lawyer and aspiring politician was uncertain and tentative.

He was well aware that he could be considered homely, with his hawkish face, coarse black hair that he didn't bother to comb, ears that were too large, and sad, sad eyes. At 6'4", he was especially tall, and gangly and awkward in the bargain. He cared nothing for clothes, his socks rarely matched, and his patched pants usually rose well above his size-14 shoes.

Although he made friends easily with men, his attitude toward the ladies was infinitely more complex and confusing. Their mere presence made him painfully aware of how poor and uneducated he was, which made him feel unsure, insecure, and decidedly unsophisticated. One time, he entered a room filled with girls and exclaimed, *"Oh boys, how clean these girls look."*

Young Lincoln's first grand passion was reportedly with Ann Rutledge. Her father owned the tavern where Lincoln boarded in 1831, when he first arrived in New Salem. Villagers described Ann, 18, as kindhearted, gentle, of good character, winsome, and comely—in fact, the prettiest girl in New Salem. Her needlework was considered a wonder, and it was no wonder she had more than her share of suitors.

Ann became engaged to a man who told her he had run away from home hoping to earn enough money to pay off his father's debts. Having succeeded in that endeavor, he was going to return and rescue his destitute family. He would write and come for Ann soon. His first letters explained that his father was ill, and therefore he would be delayed. Subsequent letters were unsatisfactory and infrequent until, inexplicably, they stopped coming. Ann did not hear from him for more than a year.

Some villagers say that Abraham courted Ann and they became engaged during that time. Ann, however, refused to marry him because she felt duty bound to explain the situation to her fiancé when he returned; they would have to wait.

In the summer of 1835, Ann came down with a mild fever; her condition worsened, and she died of what was thought to be brain fever.

Some said she died of a broken heart because of the unbearable pressure of her untenable situation. They say she summoned Abraham to her bedside days before she died.

Abraham was devastated and became despondent, lapsing into a disconsolate and melancholy state. The sudden loss of his first true love plunged him down a bottomless well of gloom and grief. Friends feared that his reason was in danger and maintained a constant vigil to ensure that he did not take his own life.

Not all of the residents of New Salem agreed with this recounting, however. They questioned the extent of Abraham's relationship with Ann and attributed his admittedly woeful mental and physical condition at the time to his habitual overwork and general melancholy nature.

Sadly, in the absence of letters or diaries from either party, the full truth cannot be known with certainty and their relationship must remain, for now, a question mark.

A year after Ann Rutledge died, Lincoln, unthinkingly and half in jest, agreed to marry the sister of a friend. He had met 28-year-old Mary Owens a few years earlier when she came from Kentucky to visit her sister in New Salem. Mary's family was wealthy and she was sophisticated and outgoing. Lincoln found her to be intelligent, well educated, and handsome, although a little overweight.

When Mary Owens returned to New Salem, she appeared to have put on yet more weight—some observers called her "portly." Lincoln, who could be cruel, was even less charitable: "*. . . skin too full of fat to permit its contraction into wrinkles . . .*"

Although probably not formally engaged, the two of them had, at the very least, an unspoken, informal understanding.

Lincoln, regretting his rashness, felt trapped and wanted, somehow, to end the relationship.

Over the summer of 1837, they courted but didn't get along very well. Mary Owens was put off by his rough, unsophisticated, and unchivalrous manner. Since Lincoln was trying to make himself as unappealing as possible, he might have been acting like this on purpose.

Lincoln not only wanted the relationship to end, but he wanted to appear blameless. Hoping to convince Mary Owens that it was her idea, he wrote a very peculiar letter:

"*. . . for the purpose of making the matter as plain as possible, I now say, that you can drop the subject, dismiss your thoughts if you ever had any, from me forever, and leave this letter unanswered without calling forth one accusing murmur from me. . . .*

"*Do not understand by this that I wish to cut your acquaintance. I mean no such thing. What I do wish is that our further acquaintance shall depend upon yourself. If such further acquaintance would contribute nothing to your happiness, I am sure it would not mine. If you feel yourself in any degree bound to me, I am now willing to release you, provided you wish it. . . .*"

*Mary Owens*

Mary Owens did not answer his letter, and the relationship ended.

Two years later, Lincoln, 30, met 21-year-old Mary Todd, the daughter of a Lexington, Kentucky, merchant and banker. Mary grew up surrounded by wealth and slaves who did all the chores. Well educated at the fanciest and most fashionable girls' schools, she was witty, intelligent, charming (when she wanted to be), and cultured (she could read and speak French).

She met Abraham Lincoln at one of the frequent parties that her sister and brother-in-law, Elizabeth and Ninian Edwards, gave at their hilltop mansion. Joshua Speed and John Stuart were frequent guests there (John and Mary were distant cousins). Now that Springfield was the state capital, the eligible bachelors associated with the government attracted a like number of equally eligible young ladies. Pretty, pert Mary Todd was one of the most sought after.

Mary Todd Lincoln

Lincoln was charmed by her: her soft skin, light-brown hair, the low necklines of the ball gowns that displayed her ample bosom, her spirited and independent nature, and her penchant for saying what was on her mind. She certainly wasn't like anyone Lincoln had ever met and wasn't a snob, like so many of the Springfield girls. (Not that he had met many: *"I have been spoken to by but one woman since I've been here, and should not have been by her, if she could have avoided it."*)

Astonishingly, Mary seemed to be genuinely interested in *him*.

He *was* different: He didn't smoke, drink, or swear like the others, and she found his shyness refreshing. They talked easily, with Mary doing most of the talking, which was fine with the usually (around females) tongue-tied Lincoln. She liked how he listened and considered everything she said. They liked the same poetry and had similar political views, no small matter for both.

Mary, too, had lost her mother when she was young. Unlike Lincoln, however, Mary disliked her stepmother intensely. She berated Mary about not attending church and not wearing more appropriate clothes, while Mary retaliated by putting salt in her coffee. Mary's inability to live in the same house with her stepmother was the reason for the extended stay with her sister in Springfield.

Mary Todd liked that Lincoln was ambitious and already had a reputation as a young politician on the rise. She loved politics and the power that came with it. She wanted to be a part of that world and knew she could only do it through an alliance with a man. For years, she had dated up-and-coming politicians and had bragged to her friends that some day she would marry the man who would become president of the United States.

During the spring and summer of 1840, they saw each other at the many parties, get-togethers, and evenings that were part of the lively Springfield social scene.

By December, they were engaged.

When Mary's brother-in-law and sister were notified, they voiced their strong disapproval. The Edwardses considered themselves Mary's surrogate parents and took their responsibilities seriously. They had tolerated her courtship, but marriage was something else. Lincoln was simply not of the same background and belonged to a different, lower class. (*For God, one 'd' is enough, but the Todds need two,* Lincoln quipped.) They informed Mary that Lincoln was not allowed to call.

Lincoln was having grave doubts—even before this dramatic news. Where would they live? On what? He didn't earn enough to support a wife, especially someone used to a life of comfort and privilege like Mary Todd. He had no savings and still had unpaid bills, debts from his failed general store back in New Salem.

Besides, he simply didn't feel he was worthy: *"I can never be satisfied with anyone who would be block-head enough to have me."*

And he wasn't the only one with doubts; Mary had some of her own. She was 23 and it was time to get married, but she had many choices. Was this Lincoln the right one? Was she really ready to exchange the exhilarating and exciting life of an attractive single woman for the responsibility of marriage and motherhood?

In January 1841, they agreed to break off the engagement.

Lincoln took to bed for a week, seeing his physician frequently and writing to Stuart:

*"Whether I shall ever be better I cannot tell; I awfully forebode I shall not. To remain as I am is impossible. I must die or be better, it appears to me."*

Everything seemed to be happening at once. Joshua Speed was getting married, leaving the store and Springfield, which meant leaving Lincoln homeless and with one less friend.

*"I am now the most miserable man living. If what I feel were equally distributed to the whole human family, there would not be one cheerful face on the earth,"* he told Stuart in late July.

Abraham and Mary's separation was the talk of the town. For a while, they stayed away from each other, somewhat difficult as they traveled in the same social circle. Lincoln visited Speed at his Louisville, Kentucky, estate, where he got some much-needed rest and encouraging advice from his ex-roommate.

THE PEOPLE OF THE STATE OF ILLINOIS.
To any Minister of the Gospel, or other authorised Person—GREETING.
THESE are to License and permit you to join in the holy bands of Matrimony Abraham Lincoln and Mary Todd of the County of Sangamon and State of Illinois, and for so doing, this shall be your sufficient warrant.

Finally, in the summer of 1842, a mutual friend intervened and invited Mary and Abraham to a social function. Each accepted, and the romance was rekindled. Lincoln

*The newlyweds' first home, the Globe Tavern*

proposed, again, and Mary accepted, again. They met clandestinely at the houses of friends, and she said nothing to the Edwardses until the morning of the wedding. Mary's brother-in-law had warmed to Lincoln, so he and his wife, when faced with Mary's well-known stubborn nature, gave in and offered their home for a hastily arranged ceremony.

The son of one of Lincoln's friends, seeing him dressing, asked where he was going:

*"To hell, I reckon,"* the soon-to-be groom replied.

He gave Mary a gold ring inscribed "Love is Eternal." Lincoln was 33 and Mary 9 years younger. Neither of their parents attended (and Lincoln's didn't even know about it for quite a while).

Four days after the wedding, Lincoln wrote:

*"Nothing new here, except my marrying, which to me is a matter of profound wonder."*

Mr. and Mrs. Lincoln rented an 8' x 14' room on the second floor of the second-rate Globe Tavern. Meals were served downstairs in the communal dining room. The accommodations suited the undemanding Lincoln just fine but were well below Mary's standards.

On August 1, 1843, nine months after the wedding, their first child, Robert, was born.

In January, they bought a small house, and two years later, Edward, "Eddie," joined the family.

Mary did all the cooking, cleaning, washing, and ironing. She pumped the water from the well, carried it back to the house for drinking, and heated it for cooking (if her husband remembered to keep the fire going). It was the first time she didn't have servants or slaves to do these things for her.

Mary did have time on her hands, thanks, primarily, to her sister. Elizabeth Edwards, perched high atop the Springfield social ladder, considered Mary's marriage a comedown and her new husband unsuitable and inferior in every way. He came from a lower social class, lacked education, was unsophisticated, used indelicate language, and had a rough, rustic manner. Elizabeth and her friends banished Mary from their social circle. For someone as lively, garrulous, and outgoing as Mary Todd, her sister's attitude proved to be a weighty and unwelcome burden during the early months of her marriage.

Caring for her young children, especially Eddie, who was sickly, took endless hours and an enormous amount of energy. She tried to discipline them, especially Robert, who needed it, but had no help from her indulgent husband. Mary worried night and day about their health (when they swallowed something that might be dangerous) and their safety (if they strayed too far and long from her sight).

Constantly exhausted, tense, and nervous, she argued with everyone: workers, neighbors, street vendors (over the price of ice and strawberries), and (as soon as they could afford one) the maid.

Lincoln, who now referred to his wife as "Molly" or "Mother" (he was "Mr. Lincoln" or "Father"), endured her temper tantrums with patience and understanding.

Once, Mary burst into the room while her husband was in the middle of a discussion with a fellow lawyer. She yelled at him about neglecting to do an errand. Although Lincoln promised he would do it the first chance he got, Mary continued to complain about how she was treated and strode out of the room, slamming the door behind her. The lawyer, startled by Mary's behavior, said something to Lincoln. Lincoln laughed and told the man:

*"Why, if you knew how much good that little eruption did, what a relief it was to her, and if you knew her as well as I do, you would be glad she had an opportunity to explode."*

He cared for her when she took to bed with one of her frequent, violent headaches, made excuses for her to the neighbors who gossiped about her, and accepted her apologies, which invariably followed each explosion. Although they were devoted to each other, they argued with increasing frequency and intensity over the years.

Lincoln's eccentric personality also played a role. He could be cold, moody, and distant, sitting for hours in his rocking chair, silently staring off into space. Mary had no way of knowing if he was pondering the meaning of life or just mulling over a complex law case.

Lincoln was not an easy man to live with, and much of the time, he wasn't even home.

He was back at work the Monday morning after the wedding, putting in long hours and was often away riding the circuit.

The Wedding - November 4, 1842
"Love is Eternal"

*Scene outside Illinois Courthouse when court was in session*

In order to hear legal cases in the towns and villages outside of Springfield, the judge visited each county in rotation—a 12,000-square-mile area. Springfield lawyers, looking for work, followed. They would arrive over the weekend, meet their new clients and the local lawyers who wanted their expertise, and quickly get to work on the paperwork so they would be ready when court convened on Monday morning.

The cases were widely debated and argued by the local citizens. When the judge and the lawyers from the big city arrived, they were greeted like members of a traveling carnival; it was the big event of the year. They stayed in each county seat from two days to two weeks. It took ten weeks to complete the circuit. A few months later, the judge and the lawyers would head out again to hear whatever cases had developed in the interim. Lincoln was one of the few lawyers who would go out twice a year.

Rising at dawn and saddling up Old Tom, or hitching him to his buggy, Lincoln traveled with a change of clothes, some legal papers, and a book in his saddlebags. The trails he went on—

little more than paths—were muddy during the spring thaw and treacherous in the unforgiving Midwest winter. He swam his horse across swollen streams when the bridges had been washed away by torrential rains and persevered through sleet and snow, with buffalo robes and blankets to protect him. He would ride for hours without seeing a soul or a man-made structure. Sometimes, even after traveling all day, he was unable to reach his destination and had to hope for a friendly farmhouse.

Upon arrival, he frequently slept in a tavern room with 20 other lawyers, two or three to a bed. Breakfast was usually bad and the coffee always.

Caring little where he slept and less about what he ate, Lincoln took to life on the circuit better than most. Although he missed his family, he enjoyed the solitude the long hours of solo traveling provided and the conviviality and brotherhood available upon arrival.

Lincoln earned a reputation for integrity and fairness. When the judge of the Eighth District was called away from the bench, he would ask Lincoln to preside over the court in his place. With an eye to his future, the always ambitious Lincoln was getting to know thousands of voters by name.

Back in Springfield, his law practice was changing. In 1841, he and Stuart (who had been away in Congress) dissolved their partnership. Lincoln joined Stephen Logan, who, like Stuart, was a prominent Springfield attorney. Logan was methodical and meticulous, a good influence on Lincoln, who disliked routine paperwork and tedious record keeping.

In 1844, Lincoln and Logan ended their partnership, and Lincoln took on William Herndon. Almost ten years younger than Lincoln, Herndon had been a clerk in Joshua Speed's grocery store.

Herndon was, like Lincoln, "informal," and their offices reflected it. There was a stove, a desk with lots of little cubbies, a bookcase filled with law books, two tables (a long one and a short one placed together to form a T), some chairs, and an old sofa.

Lincoln, who arrived most mornings at nine, could usually be found stretched out on the sofa, one leg propped up on a pulled-over chair, or just up on the wall, devouring the newspapers. He insisted, much to Herndon's annoyance, on reading them aloud:

*"When I read aloud two senses catch the idea: first, I see what I read; second, I hear it, and therefore can remember it better."*

The bare, unswept floor was covered with dust mixed with the cherry pits and orange seeds that Lincoln spat out while he munched his lunch: milk, a biscuit, some fruit. The windows went unwashed (and only looked out on an alley, anyway) and papers were piled all over the floor or in a bundle marked by Lincoln: *"When you can't find it anywhere else, look into this."*

Herndon was a surprise choice. Lincoln could have picked any one of the more experienced Springfield lawyers who were available to him. Herndon was not only young, but known to be careless and extreme in everything, including his anti-slavery, abolitionist views.

But Lincoln had his reasons. With Stuart and Logan, he had been the junior partner. With Herndon, although they split fees 50-50, Lincoln would be the senior of the two. More importantly, Herndon was connected to a group of younger up-and-coming politicians in town, and Lincoln thought that might benefit him in the not-too-distant future.

Herndon admired his new partner and appreciated his sage advice:

*"The leading rule for the lawyer, as for the man of every calling, is diligence."*

*". . . Don't shoot high—aim lower and the common people will understand you. They are the ones you want to reach."*

Lincoln called him "Billy" and he called Lincoln "Mr. Lincoln."

They took on a wide variety of cases: bankruptcy, slander (getting a penny for one client), divorce, embezzlement, assault and battery, and murder. They represented people from every social and economic class, the guilty as well as the innocent. Fees were reasonable, and some so small they accepted groceries, produce, and poultry in return for their services. Sometimes, Lincoln returned money he received if he thought it was too much.

Lincoln's courtroom style was folksy and friendly, but never sentimental. He used plain language to simplify the most complex issues. He spoke to the jurors, many of whom he knew from his days as postmaster and surveyor, in a conversational tone, weaving his talk with humor.

He rarely raised objections and would not contend minor points. But he could be ruthless and relentless when it came to the ones he considered critical.

By 1843, 34-year-old Abraham Lincoln was feeling more confident professionally and politically with each passing week. Lincoln believed the time was right to run for a seat in the U.S. Congress. He was unable, however, to get the backing he needed within his own party, and his campaign never got off the ground.

He tried again and, in August 1846, was elected. (His friends had raised 200 dollars for his campaign—he returned all but 75 cents unused.)

Thirty-seven-year-old Abraham Lincoln was going to Washington.

*Pennsylvania Ave., Washington, D.C., circa 1843*

In October 1847, the Lincolns leased their Springfield home and sold what they could not store. They stayed three weeks in Lexington, Kentucky. (Mary's father had come to like his new son-in-law—using him for a legal matter and giving the young couple money from time to time). Then they traveled by stage, steamer, and railroad, arriving ten days later in the nation's capital (pop: 40,000, including 8,000 free blacks and 2,000 slaves).

Mansions and museums stood side by side with shacks. The sidewalks were dirt and gravel, and clouds of dust rose up from the traffic on the unpaved streets, which were littered with garbage. Pigs, geese, and chickens roamed free. In the winter, the mud was so deep that boys earned tips from men with shiny boots and ladies with long dresses who they escorted safely across on planks. In the summer, the malaria-bearing mosquitoes were so lethal that those citizens who could afford to left the city.

The Lincolns took a single room in a boardinghouse with eight other Congressmen (the unfinished Capitol building could be seen from one of the windows).

Lincoln entertained everyone at mealtimes with his bottomless well of humorous and pointed stories, and bowled (badly but enthusiastically) at a nearby hotel. He was the only one who had brought his wife, and Mary felt lonely and out of place. She rarely ventured from her room.

They argued, as they had back in Springfield, and after three months, Mary left. She took four-year-old Robert and Eddie, who was almost two, and went south to Lexington to visit with their grandfather.

Lincoln was lonely without his family and worried in his letters that Bob and Eddie would forget him. Mary wrote that she missed him also, but when he returned to Washington for the second session, she remained back home in Springfield with the children.

Lincoln, freed from the responsibility of family, worked long and hard, rarely missing a roll call. However, when his term was up, he was unable to run again because of his party's principle of rotation in office. He tried to get appointed to a well-paid, somewhat powerful government position that was available, but was unsuccessful.

By the summer of 1849, a disappointed Abraham Lincoln was back home in Springfield, forced to return to private practice—his political future uncertain.

On the morning of February 1, 1850, Eddie, who had been gravely ill for weeks, died of consumption.

His parents had nursed him day and night, but there was nothing they could do.

Mary collapsed in shock and remained in her bedroom for weeks, crying constantly. She ate little and came out only when pressed by her husband. She turned to religion for solace, something her spiritual, but skeptical husband could not do. She would never be the same.

Lincoln, too, was devastated but suffered silently, as was his way, saying only, *"We miss him very much."*

Eleven months after Eddie's death, in December 1850, William—soon to be called "Willie"—was born.

A month later, Lincoln's father died. Lincoln refused to go to his deathbed, writing his stepbrother: *"Say to him that if we could meet now, it is doubtful whether it would not be more painful than pleasant. . . ."*

He did not attend the funeral.

In April 1853, Thomas (named, curiously, after Lincoln's father) joined the family. They called him "Tad" because he looked like a tadpole.

Lincoln, who was never close with Robert (due, in part, to Lincoln's being away much of the time when the boy was young), spent time with his young boys. Willie was affectionate and intelligent, and liked to read. Tad had a lisp because of a cleft palette, which endeared him even more to his father.

Lincoln liked to tickle the boys, toss them in the air, and roll around on the floor with them. He brought them into the office on Sundays, while their mother was at church, and allowed them to pull the law books down from the bookcases, turn over the inkwells, throw pencils into the spittoon, and empty the ash bucket all over the floor. Even more permissive since Eddie died, Lincoln hardly noticed.

*Mr. and Mrs. Lincoln's First Photographs taken in 1846 in Springfield, Illinois*

# CANDIDATE

## (1854-1860)

### SLAVERY · DEBATES · NATIONAL PROMINENCE · NOMINATION ELECTION

By the mid-1850s, Lincoln had become one of Illinois's top attorneys and his practice had changed. He and Herndon now added banks, insurance and gas companies, and railroads to their client list. They were involved in patent and maritime law and tried cases in Chicago, the Illinois Supreme Court, the federal courts, and the U.S. Supreme Court.

Lincoln was doing better financially, making investments and sending money periodically to his stepmother. He wasn't forgetting his old friends. When Jack Armstrong's widow asked if he would take her son's case, he did, even though she didn't have any money to pay him. The boy was accused of killing someone late one night. The prosecution's eyewitness said he could positively identify the Armstrong boy because of the bright moonlight.

Lincoln, who always took pains picking a jury (believing that fat men

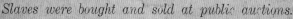

*Slaves were bought and sold at public auctions.*

could easily be swayed and people with high foreheads couldn't), made certain most of the jurors were young men under 30 who would identify with his client. The fact that he knew many of their fathers didn't hurt.

During the trial, Lincoln produced an almanac that proved the moon had almost set by the time the killing took place, so there wasn't nearly enough light to identify the assailant.

Jack Armstrong's son was acquitted.

During this time, Lincoln stayed away from politics, feeling his future was bleak. He continued to read the newspapers and talk with his colleagues about the news coming out of the nation's capital. One thing was certain: The question of slavery was becoming more troubling with each passing day.

———

The history of slavery in the United States began in 1619, when the first Africans were brought here against their will. The issue was not addressed—a decision in itself—by the American Revolution or the Declaration of Independence, which said *"all men are created equal,"* but meant all white men. The Founding Fathers and the leaders of the 13 colonies who formed the United States were in conflict about the issue, so slavery remained and the question of its future was left unaddressed.

In 1820, the Missouri Compromise settled, to a degree, the question of slavery's expansion into the western territories. It stipulated that a line be drawn east-west, at latitude 36°30'. Below that line, slavery would be allowed; above it, the new territories or states would be free of slavery. It was an uneasy and temporary truce.

In May 1854, the Kansas-Nebraska Act was signed into law, superseding the Missouri Compromise and replacing the line with the concept of popular sovereignty. This allowed the citizens of each territory to determine by vote whether they wanted to allow slavery or not.

The Kansas-Nebraska Act reignited the still-smoldering question of the future of slavery. The author of the bill and the champion of popular sovereignty was the powerful, two-time Illinois Senator Stephen Douglas. Douglas decided to speak across the state in defense of the now-controversial idea of popular sovereignty.

Five feet four inches tall, Douglas was known as the "Little Giant." Cocky, with a lion-like mane of black hair and a deep, booming voice, the cigar-smoking Douglas was as feisty as he was short. He and Stuart, Lincoln's former law partner, had a fight during which Douglas bit Stuart severely enough to leave a scar. Douglas had been, before Lincoln, one of Mary Todd's unsuccessful suitors.

Lincoln had, over the course of his life, numerous encounters with the stark reality of slavery: when he went down to New Orleans on the flatboat; in Kentucky, where he saw slave auctions and chained slave gangs heading south to the cotton fields; and in the nation's capital, where he encountered slave-holding pens.

Mary Todd, growing up in Lexington, Kentucky, had even more intimate knowledge of slavery. She was aware that one of her family's slaves had marked the fence so that people would know to come to their back door late at night. She knew they were helping other slaves escape to the North.

She had also heard about her neighbor, Mrs. Turner, and how she had beaten six slaves to death and crippled one by throwing him out the window. Mary had been told that one of the slaves, who had taken enough abuse, had strangled Turner to death.

Like many others, Lincoln was shaken by the Kansas-Nebraska Act. It signaled, he believed, a disturbing shift. Southern leaders were no longer content that slavery be allowed to remain where it existed. They, along with Douglas and the Democratic party, were using popular sovereignty to allow slavery to expand along with the westward expansion of the country.

Lincoln believed the Kansas-Nebraska Act would solve nothing, bring further divisiveness, and result in widespread violence.

He decided to confront Douglas, whom he had debated years before. Genuinely concerned, while perceiving it as an opportunity to revive his stalled political career, Lincoln announced he would follow Douglas wherever he spoke and present the opposing view.

In October 1854, he gave a three-hour speech at the Springfield State Fair that presented his thoughts on this most complex and contentious issue in a forthright, coherent, and heartfelt manner.

*"I hate it because of the monstrous injustice of slavery itself. I hate it because it deprives our republican example of its vast influence in the world—enables the enemies of free institutions, with plausibility, to . . . doubt our sincerity.*

*". . . If all earthly power were given me, I should not know what to do, as to the existing institution. My first impulse would be to free all the slaves, and send them to Liberia—to their own native land. But a moment's reflection would convince me that, in the long run, its sudden execution is impossible.*

*". . . What next?—Free them, and make them politically and socially our equals? My own feelings will not admit of this; and if mine would, we well know that those of*

*the great mass of white people will not.*

*"When the white man governs himself, that is self-government; but when he governs*

John Brown

John Brown from daguerreotype loaned me by Annie Brown. 494 Mt Ave. S.W. WASHINGTON D.C. Regarded as the best picture by the family

*himself, and also governs another man, that is more than self-government—that is despotism.*

*". . . My ancient faith teaches me that 'all men are created equal'; and that there can be no moral right in connection with one man's making a slave of another.*

*". . . No man is good enough to govern another man, without that other's consent. I say this is the leading principle . . . of . . . American republicanism.*

*". . . Repeal the Missouri compromise— repeal all compromises. Repeal the declaration of independence—repeal all past history, you still cannot repeal human nature. It still will be the abundance of man's heart, that slavery extension is wrong; and*

*out of the abundance of his heart, his mouth will continue to speak."*

In November 1854, Lincoln was elected to the Illinois State Legislature, but resigned his seat (as he was required to do), so that he could campaign for the U.S. Senate. He lost, due to some questionable interparty maneuvering, but appeared magnanimous in defeat. High-strung, fiery Mary did not. The wife of the man who beat Lincoln had been her bridesmaid and a lifelong friend. Mary never spoke to her again.

———————————

As Lincoln feared, violence came to Kansas, a territory that lacked any real law and order. Southern pro-slavery forces were intent on making Kansas a slave state—by force if necessary. They brought nonresidents by the thousands illegally across the border to vote for candidates who supported slavery. Anti-slavery forces responded as both sides armed themselves with shotguns, rifles, pistols, knives, and ropes for hanging their enemies.

Abolitionist John Brown, along with his four sons and two others, killed five pro-slavery men with swords in retaliation for a previous killing of anti-slavery men.

Civil war had broken out in what was now being called "Bleeding Kansas."

There was blood on the Senate floor as well.

Arrogant and sophisticated, Harvard-educated Massachusetts Sen. Charles Sumner was an outspoken opponent of slavery. In May 1856, he delivered a long, purposely provocative speech denouncing slave owners, in particular Andrew Butler, his fellow senator from South Carolina.

Preston Brooks, Butler's nephew and himself a congressman from that same state, approached Sumner's desk and began beating him unmercifully with a cane as Sumner was writing.

Brooks explained that he had attacked Sumner while he was sitting, because if Sumner, the bigger of the two, had stood up, he would have been forced to shoot and kill him and he only wanted to injure him.

Brooks later received canes from fellow Southerners who suggested he use them on any members of Congress who also had the nerve to speak out against slavery.

That same year, people from various political parties and interest groups, provoked by the Kansas-Nebraska Act, formed the Republican Party, which was dedicated to opposing any further extension of slavery. Lincoln was the keynote speaker at the Illinois Republican Convention and runner-up for the vice presidential nomination. Must be *"some other Lincoln,"* he was heard to say.

In March 1857, the Supreme Court handed down the *Dred Scott* decision. According to the chief justice, the Founding Fathers had not included black people in their Declaration of Independence. They were not, therefore, citizens of the United States and had no rights.

Lincoln, like many others, was shocked by the *Dred Scott* decision, which was a major setback for the anti-slavery advocates.

In June 1858, the Republicans nominated him to run against Democratic Senator Douglas. He worked hard on his acceptance speech, knowing what an important opportunity it was. Scribbling on the backs of envelopes or on stray pieces of paper that he stored in his tall hat, he rewrote and revised until he was satisfied.

The speech presented Lincoln's unblinking look at what was becoming a national catastrophe. In simple, yet eloquent language, he cut to the very heart of the matter:

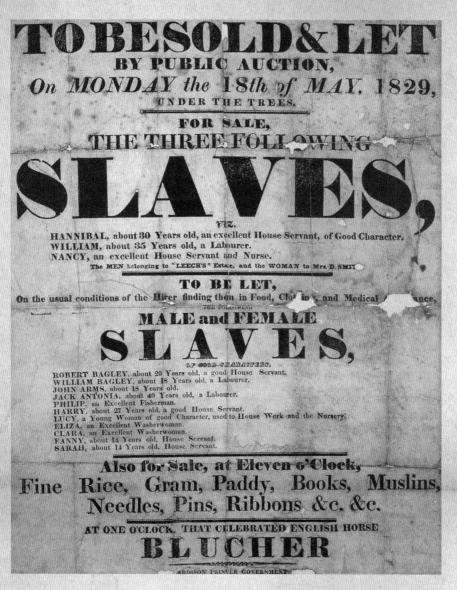

**TO BE SOLD & LET**
BY PUBLIC AUCTION,
On MONDAY the 18th of MAY, 1829,
UNDER THE TREES.
FOR SALE,
THE THREE FOLLOWING
**SLAVES,**
VIZ.
HANNIBAL, about 30 Years old, an excellent House Servant, of Good Character.
WILLIAM, about 35 Years old, a Labourer.
NANCY, an excellent House Servant and Nurse.
The MEN belonging to "LEECH'S" Estate, and the WOMAN to Mrs. D. SMIT

**TO BE LET,**
On the usual conditions of the Hirer finding them in Food, Clothing, and Medical
THE FOLLOWING
**MALE and FEMALE**
**SLAVES,**
OF GOOD CHARACTERS,
ROBERT BAGLEY, about 20 Years old, a good House Servant.
WILLIAM BAGLEY, about 18 Years old, a Labourer.
JOHN ARMS, about 18 Years old.
JACK ANTONIA, about 40 Years old, a Labourer.
PHILIP, an Excellent Fisherman.
HARRY, about 27 Years old, a good House Servant.
LUCY, a Young Woman of good Character, used to House Work and the Nursery.
ELIZA, an Excellent Washerwoman.
CLARA, an Excellent Washerwoman.
FANNY, about 14 Years old, House Servant.
SARAH, about 14 Years old, House Servant.

**Also for Sale, at Eleven o'Clock,**
**Fine Rice, Gram, Paddy, Books, Muslins,**
**Needles, Pins, Ribbons &c. &c.**
AT ONE O'CLOCK, THAT CELEBRATED ENGLISH HORSE
**BLUCHER**
ADDISON PRINTER GOVERNMENT

*"If we could first know where we are, and whether we are tending, we could better judge what to do, and how to do it.*

*"We are now far into the fifth year, since a policy was initiated, with the avowed object, and confident promise, of putting an end to slavery agitation.*

*"Under the present operation of that policy, that agitation has not only, not ceased, but has constantly augmented.*

*"In my opinion, it will not cease, until a crisis shall have been reached and passed.*

*"'A house divided against itself cannot stand.'*

*"I believe this government cannot endure, permanently half slave and half free.*

*"I do not expect the Union will be dissolved—I do not expect the house to fall—but I do expect it will cease to be divided.*

*"It will become all one thing, or all the other."*

Lincoln believed the Republican Party, if it continued to increase and unify its membership, might have some success in the upcoming national elections.

He challenged the Little Giant to a series of 50 debates. Douglas, never one to back down from a fight, even if it was politically the right thing to do, agreed to seven. They debated in the afternoons and in the evenings, in the blazing sun and in the cold rain. Crowds numbered in the thousands, as many as 15,000 in the larger towns.

There were brass bands, glee clubs, torchlight processions, horse-drawn wagons decorated with bunting, and pretty girls bearing flowers.

Farmers and their families came from miles around, some simply walking or on horseback, others riding in buggies or wagons. At times, there were so many of them they clogged the roads and raised huge clouds of dust. They also came by canal boat and the railroads that offered reduced excursion fares. Fourteen railway cars brought people out from Chicago—some in the brand-new sleeper cars.

Shopkeepers dressed their windows for the occasion and citizens hung flags from their porches. Banners were draped from buildings and across the main street— some featuring life-size likenesses of the two combatants. In one town, Charleston, an 80-foot-long banner showed young Abe, back in Kentucky, driving his yoked oxen.

Douglas draped his stocky frame in fine suits made of blue linen and adorned with silver buttons. He moved with surprising grace. His bass voice commanded attention, as did his sophistication and his beautiful wife, who accompanied him everywhere.

Lincoln, although appearing to stoop when he stood and slouch when he walked, seemed even taller than his 6'4". He wore his everyday clothes, as if to say this was nothing special and to emphasize his roots among the common man in the audience. He moved awkwardly, his high-pitched tenor voice sounding shrill at times. Mary attended only the last debate.

In addition to the seven debates, they spoke nearly every day for four months. Douglas traveled more than 5,000 miles and gave 130 speeches and became so hoarse that in the end he could barely be heard. Lincoln, who grew stronger, gave 63 speeches and traveled more than 4,000 miles.

In the end, what remained were their opposing views on the meaning of the American Revolution and equality.

The debates made the distinction between the philosophies these two men represented very clear.

The advocates for each claimed victory and the nation's newspapers reported on the debates, often printing them in their entirety. *The New York Times* considered the debates a reflection of national concern.

The election results were close, but Lincoln failed to unseat Douglas.

The debates had, however, more far-reaching results than deciding who would represent Illinois in the Senate. They made Abraham Lincoln a nationally known political figure.

Always striving to strike the appropriate note, Lincoln took the high road:

*"It gave me a hearing on the great and durable question of the age, which I could have had in no other way; and though I now sink out of view, and shall be forgotten, I believe that I have made some marks which will tell for the cause of liberty long after I am gone."*

*"The fight must go on. The cause of civil liberty must not be surrendered at the end of one, or even, one hundred defeats."*

Abraham Lincoln spent a great deal of his time in 1859 delivering speeches in Illinois and the surrounding states, part of a well-thought-out plan to advertise himself and the new Republican Party.

In one speech he addressed the people of the South:

*Federal Arsenal, Harper's Ferry, Virginia*

"*. . . A warning about your repeated threats to split up the Union if we win the Presidency. How will disunion help you? If you secede, you will no longer enjoy the protection of the Constitution; we will no longer be obligated to return your fugitive slaves. What will you do, build a wall between us? Make war on us? You are brave and gallant, but man for man you are no braver than we are, and we outnumber you. You can't master us, and since you can't, secession and war would be the worst of follies. . . .*"

*Abraham Lincoln*

In mid-October, John Brown attacked the federal arsenal in Harper's Ferry, Virginia. He and 18 followers (including five blacks), took prisoners and freed slaves, telling them to spread the word that all slaves should rise up.

The shooting went on for two days until Col. Robert E. Lee, commanding 80 marines, captured Brown and killed and captured a number of his men.

People in the North were stunned, but in the South the citizenry was nearly frantic. Brown's audacious raid at Harper's Ferry convinced them that Northern abolitionists were heading south with arms for the slaves, preaching violence and death to white people. They were certain a full-scale slave uprising was upon them.

In February 1860, wearing a new black suit, Lincoln traveled to New York City, where he spoke at Cooper Union. Despite a severe snowstorm, 1,500 people attended.

He ended his speech saying:

★ ★ ★ ★ ★ ★ ★ ★ ★ ★ ★ ★ ★

**"Let us have faith that right makes might, and in that faith, let us, to the end, dare to do our duty as we understand it."**

★ ★ ★ ★ ★ ★ ★ ★ ★ ★ ★ ★ ★

He received a standing ovation as the audience members waved hats and handkerchiefs and rushed up to shake his hand and congratulate him. The New York morning papers published the entire speech.

Back home in Illinois, the Cooper Union speech and its enthusiastic reception back east, in the big city, increased Lincoln's stature.

By the spring of 1860, Lincoln was ready to make his move (*"I will be frank. The taste is in my mouth"*). After a secret meeting in Springfield, his campaign team began working behind the scenes, their eyes on the upcoming Republican National Convention being held in nearby Chicago.

They published Lincoln-Douglas debate books (1 dollar hardcover and 50 cents paperback), which became a best seller, and made the Cooper Union speech available for a penny.

Securing the nomination for their candidate was problematic. The two front-runners were adroit, experienced political insiders who were far better known than Lincoln. But that was the good news as well.

Unlike them, Lincoln was considered a political outsider, which was in his favor. He had no record to defend, no radical statements to disavow, and no real enemies. In addition, the two front-runners were suspected of being unable to win in November.

Lincoln's aides, most seasoned politicians and all loyal to him, worked hard at the Republican convention. They canvassed delegates night and day, convincing, cajoling, prodding, praising, and flattering—but refusing to make any promises. *"Make no contracts that will bind me,"* Lincoln had instructed. Reluctantly, he remained behind in Springfield, appearing not to be a candidate, as tradition dictated. They kept him informed of their progress via telegram:

**"We are quiet but moving heaven & Earth. Nothing will beat us but old fogy politicians."**

**"Don't be frightened. Keep cool. Things working."**

**"Am very hopeful. Don't be excited. Nearly dead with fatigue. Telegraph or write here very little."**

**"Dont come here for God's sake."**

When the balloting began, Lincoln was a popular second choice but a long shot to actually get the nomination. Support for the two front-runners, however, proved weak and on the third ballot, Lincoln was nominated unanimously.

Hastily-put-together campaign biographies (including one with his name spelled wrong) transformed Abraham Lincoln into "Old Abe," the "Backwoodsman," "The Self-made Man," "A Man of the People," and "Honest Abe." Lincoln didn't mind being considered a self-made man but hated being called Abe—especially Honest Abe.

*Stephen Douglas*

The biographies told the story of the candidate's log-cabin birth, dirt-poor childhood, and miraculous rise, thanks to his intelligence and diligence. It was an American success story, just as it was supposed to be, awaiting only the fairy tale ending of the presidency.

★ ★ ★ ★ ★ ★ ★ ★ ★ ★ ★ ★ ★

*"This government was made by the white man, for the benefit of white men, to be administered by white men."* –DOUGLAS

★ ★ ★ ★ ★ ★ ★ ★ ★ ★ ★ ★ ★

With the Democratic Party split over the issue of slavery into a Northern faction with Stephen Douglas as a candidate, a Southern one with John Breckinridge, and a third party further dividing the vote, Lincoln's chances were good.

On November 6, 1860, Election Day, Lincoln voted at 3:00 PM, had supper with Mary at 5:00 PM, and then went to the state house to await the news. The telegraph told the tale: Illinois, New England, Indiana, and Pennsylvania looked good. New York State's 35 electoral votes would be critical. A little after midnight, the results came in over the wire.

Lincoln received less than 40 percent of the popular vote—his opponents had one million more votes than he did. However, he carried California, Oregon, and every Northern state except New Jersey (which split with Douglas) and won 180 electoral votes, making him president-elect.

In the 15 Southern slave states, he did not receive one electoral vote. In ten, he didn't receive a single popular vote.

This, as much as anything, foretold the future for Abraham Lincoln.

*"Well, boys, your troubles are over now, mine have just begun,"* Lincoln told newsmen the day after his election.

So many people descended on Springfield that he had to move his family into the state house and hire a secretary. They all wanted something: artists for him to sit; journalists for him to talk; politicians to listen to their plans; and the rest to give them jobs and favors in return for their support, which, they explained, had gotten him elected. *"They don't want much and they get very little . . . I know how I would feel in their place."*

Lincoln met with Vice President-elect Hannibal Hamlin and other leading Republicans, and worked on his Cabinet, which he hoped to make geographically and politically balanced. He had an emotional visit with his stepmother and told Billy Herndon: *"If I live I'm coming back some time, and then we'll go right on practicing law as if nothing happened."*

In mid-February, Lincoln bid farewell to the people of Springfield:

*"My friends—No one, not in my situation, can appreciate my feelings of sadness at this parting. To this place, and the kindness of these people, I owe everything. Here I have lived a quarter of a century, and have passed from a young to an old*

*man. Here my children were born, and one is buried. I now leave, not knowing when, or whether ever, I may return."* Addressing his trunk: A. Lincoln, the White House, Washington, D.C., he departed on a 12-day, nearly 2,000-mile train trip that would take him through five Northern states to the nation's capital.

When the train stopped in Westfield, New York, Lincoln asked 11-year-old Grace Bedell to emerge from the crowd. She had written him back in October, when he was running for the presidency.

Hon A B Lincoln . . .

Dear Sir
Oct. 15, 1860

**My father has just home from the fair and brought home your picture and Mr. Hamlin's. I am a little girl only eleven years old, but want you should be President of the United States very much so I hope you wont think me very bold to write to such a great man as you are. Have you any little girls about as large as I am if so give them my love and tell her to write to me if you cannot answer this letter. I have got 4 brother's and part of them will vote for you any way and if you let your whiskers grow I will try and get the rest of them to vote for you you would look a great deal better for your face is so thin. All the ladies like whiskers and they would tease their husband's to vote for you and then you would be President. When you direct your letter dir[e]ct to Grace Bedell Westfield Chatauque County New York I must not write any more answer this letter right off Good bye**

Grace Bedell

Lincoln *had* grown a beard and wanted to thank her for the idea.

He attended parades, gave formal addresses, and spoke at official receptions and from the rear platform of the train when it stopped so he could greet the flag-waving crowds. In the three months since the election, Lincoln said nothing that would further inflame the political situation, which was deteriorating by the day.

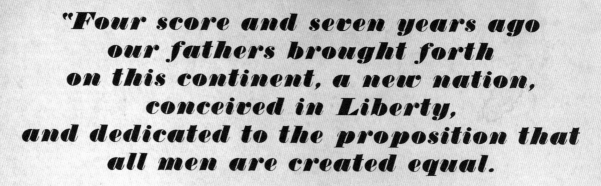

*"Four score and seven years ago
our fathers brought forth
on this continent, a new nation,
conceived in Liberty,
and dedicated to the proposition that
all men are created equal.*

*Now we are engaged in a great civil war,
testing whether that nation,
or any nation so conceived and dedicated,
can long endure."*

★ ★ ★ ★ ★ ★ ★

# 1861
# CIVIL WAR BEGINS!

## INAUGURATION · SUMTER & WAR
## LEE · SIXTH MASS. · ELLSWORTH
## BULL RUN · MARY

When Abraham Lincoln headed to the nation's capital for his inauguration as the sixteenth president of the United States, South Carolina, Mississippi, Florida, Alabama, Georgia, Louisiana, and Texas had already seceded from the Union and formed the Confederate States of America.

Lincoln did not think it would come to this:

"... This crisis is all artificial. It has no foundation in facts. It was not argued up, as the saying is, and cannot, therefore, be argued down. Let it alone and it will go down of itself."

But he was wrong; it would not "go down of itself." He underestimated the extent to which the Southern states believed they had a right to leave the Union and the depth of their determination to continue the practice of slavery.

At the end of the trip east, Lincoln was presented with irrefutable evidence that there was a plot to kill him in Baltimore, a city seething with Southern secessionist sympathy. He had been receiving hate mail and threats on his life since he was elected. Some threatened he would be killed before he reached Washington. He refused to cut his trip short but reluctantly agreed to a change of plans.

At Philadelphia, a female detective reserved space on the train for her "invalid brother."

Lincoln wore a muffler and a floppy hat that covered his face some. He was accompanied only by his friend and self-appointed bodyguard, Ward Hill Lamon, who was heavily armed (four guns, two large knives, a slingshot, and brass knuckles). They boarded the last car of the New York–Washington train. All telegraph lines had been cut as a further precaution.

In the early hours of the morning, Abraham Lincoln arrived in a sleeping berth with the curtains drawn. The Eastern press was already convinced that the first president-elect born west of the Appalachian Mountains was a provincial fool. Now hearing that he had entered Washington incognito, unannounced, and under cover of darkness, they ridiculed him as a coward.

Lincoln bore the criticism with his customary silence.

Thousands were in Washington for Lincoln's inauguration. The city's overbooked hotels, including Willard's, where the Lincolns would stay, had to bring in hundreds of extra mattresses and cots and place them in the halls, parlors, and even bathrooms to accommodate everyone. Still, hundreds walked the streets with no place to stay.

Security for the March 4 event was unprecedented and extensive. Cavalry rode double file, flanking Lincoln's carriage, and infantry marched behind. Intersections were blocked off by mounted soldiers, whose skittish horses, sensing the danger, were difficult to control. Riflemen patrolled the rooftops, their eyes trained on the windows of the buildings below. Plainclothes detectives and uniformed police mingled with the crowd, looking for anyone or anything suspicious.

The Capitol, as if mirroring the transitory state of the union, was still incomplete. The

*The Inauguration of the 16th President of the United States - March 4, 1861*

1861

arm of a giant crane swung from the skeletal dome.

Lincoln had read his inaugural address to the family earlier that day. Now dressed in his new black suit, shined black boots, stovepipe hat (which he would remove before speaking) and carrying an ebony, gold-headed cane, he looked rather presidential.

His sad face looked even graver than usual.

Speaking pointedly to the citizens of the South, he ended on a plaintive note:

*"I am loath to close. We are not enemies, but friends. We must not be enemies. Though passion may have strained, it must not break our bonds of affection. The mystic chords of memory, stretching from every battle-field, and patriot grave, to every living heart and hearthstone, all over this broad land, will yet swell the chorus of the Union, when again touched, as surely as they will be, by the better angels of our nature."*

The morning after the inauguration, President Lincoln had to confront the deepening crisis at Fort Sumter. Located in the middle of South Carolina's Charleston Harbor, Sumter was one of the last symbols of Northern military power remaining in the South. South

Carolina demanded that the garrison be abandoned and had fired on supply ships sent there months before Lincoln took office.

The War Department informed Lincoln that 20,000 men would be needed to hold the fort—an impossibility as there were only 16,000 men in the entire army. The food at Sumter was now running out, and they had to be resupplied by force or they would be forced to surrender.

Lincoln believed that further compromise would accomplish nothing: *"The tug has to come, and better now, than any time hereafter."*

Overwhelmed and uncertain, the president consulted his Cabinet and agonized over his decision. In the end, he chose to notify South Carolina that he was sending ships loaded only with provisions—no men or arms. Even so, Lincoln knew that his action was risky.

On April 11, Confederate officers demanded the surrender of Fort Sumter; the Southern-born commanding officer refused.

At 4:00 AM on April 12, Confederate batteries opened fire, continuing the constant, heavy bombardment for 34 hours.

On the morning of April 13, their food almost gone, they surrendered.

At noon on April 14, the commanding officer of Fort Sumter lowered the Stars and Stripes (which he took with him) and watched the Confederate flag being raised as he and his men evacuated the fort.

The Civil War had begun.

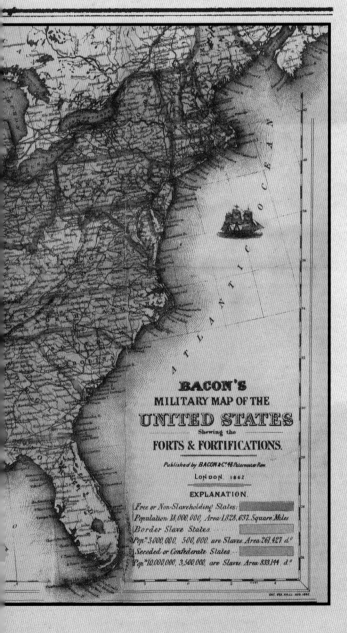

# SUMTER SURRENDERS!

## 70-Man Garrison Near Exhaustion As Food Runs Out

### Citizens Of Charleston Rejoice In Rebel Victory

### CONFEDERATE FLAG FLIES OVER FORT

### Pres. Calls For 75,000 90-Day Vols To Smother Southern Insurrection

### States Form Militia Units

Response Overwhelming As War Fever Engulfs Northern Cities

The next day, President Lincoln called for 75,000 volunteers to be sent to Washington to stop what he considered an illegal rebellion:

*"No state can, in any way lawfully, get out of the Union without the consent of the others. . . .*

*"We must settle this question now, whether in a free government the minority have the right to break up the government whenever they choose. If we fail it will go far to prove the incapability of the people to govern themselves."*

in the Mexican War and was widely considered the most capable officer in the military.

Lee refused Lincoln's offer, citing his loyalty to his state (Virginia, the largest slave state, had seceded three days after Sumter; Arkansas, North Carolina, and Tennessee would follow) and his unwillingness to fight against his family. He stated he was against secession and slavery, but was a slave owner himself. Many Southern officers had resigned and were returning home. Now, Lee joined them, riding south to Virginia, where, five days later, he took command of the Army of Northern Virginia.

Gen. Robert E. Lee

*Michigan volunteers march off to war.*

President Lincoln offered command of the Union Army to Robert E. Lee. Lee didn't smoke, drink, or swear and graduated second in his class at West Point without getting even one demerit. He was married to a descendant of George Washington and had been the superintendent of West Point. He was called by some "The Marble Model" because he was so perfect. He had performed admirably

Knowing that Washington was vulnerable to attack, Lincoln, along with the city's residents, watched and waited anxiously for the 75,000 soldiers he had summoned.

On April 19, the men of the Sixth Massachusetts regiment were passing through Baltimore on their way to Washington. The soldiers had to detrain at one point and march through the downtown area. An angry mob, carrying Confederate flags and uncontrolled by the passive police, confronted them. They threw bricks, stones, and bottles at the soldiers, who had been ordered not to respond. There were gunshots, and some had to fight their way back to the train. At least four soldiers and nine civilians were killed, and several more wounded. These were the first casualties of the Civil War.

Bloodied, bandaged, and frightened, carrying their wounded on stretchers (their dead having already been packed in ice and sent north), the men and boys of the Sixth Massachusetts regiment arrived in Washington, a city unprepared to care for them.

Baltimore officials wanted the president to stop sending soldiers headed to the nation's capital through their city:

*"Our men are not moles, and can't dig under the ground; they are not birds, and can't fly through the air,"* Lincoln replied.

Surrounded by slave states, people living in the nation's capital feared that they were about to be attacked. Shops were boarded up, buildings barricaded with sandbags and huge iron plates, hotels emptied, and homes abandoned as many fled.

At last, the troops began arriving in large numbers. Following the Confederate bombardment of Fort Sumter, hundreds and thousands—sometimes whole towns—had lined up to enlist, riding a wave of patriotic feeling. Understanding little of the cruel realities of war, they wanted to do their duty, show they were brave, defend the idea of union, and be part of what appeared to be a great adventure. As brass bands played, their neighbors cheered and waved flags, and politicians gave speeches, they marched off to war.

On the morning of May 23, Federal troops moved out of Washington, south into Virginia. The small Confederate force there fell back and the Northern soldiers occupied the town of Alexandria, only eight miles away from Washington.

A regiment of volunteers recruited from among New York City's firemen was led by 24-year-old Elmer Ellsworth.

He had been a law student in Lincoln's office and gave speeches in support of his campaign. Mary liked him as much as her husband did, and so did Willie and Tad, who he played with (and who gave the measles to him on the trip east for the inauguration). He was considered a member of the family and was like another son to the president.

Ellsworth and his men were on their way to cut the telegraph wires when they saw a Confederate flag hanging over the town's three-story hotel. The president could see one of the rebel flags from the White House.

Entering the lobby, they encountered a man dressed in civilian clothes. Ellsworth asked him about the flag, but the man said he was just a boarder and knew nothing about a flag.

Ellsworth and two of his men took down the flag. When they reentered the hotel, the man Ellsworth had spoken to was waiting. He was the owner of the hotel and a rabid secessionist. He stepped out from behind a door and shot Ellsworth through the heart with a double-barreled shotgun, killing him instantly. One of Ellsworth's men shot the hotel owner in the face and stabbed him repeatedly with his bayonet as he went down.

Lincoln, Mary, and the boys were shocked and deeply saddened by the news of Col. Ellsworth's death. He was the first commissioned officer to die in the Civil War.

Lincoln's heartfelt letter of condolence to Ellsworth's parents was the first of many he would write.

As the weeks and months passed, public opinion was increasingly insistent that the Union Army attack the Southern rebels and put an end to the war. "ON TO RICHMOND," the Confederate capital, only a hundred miles away in Virginia, demanded Northern newspapers.

Lincoln repeatedly urged his generals to attack Confederate positions. They were reluctant; more time was needed to properly discipline and train the raw recruits, they said. Lincoln, acutely aware that people were beginning to lose faith in him and the govern-

ment, replied: *"You are green, it is true. But they are green also. You are all green alike."*

On Sunday, July 21, 1861, three months after Sumter, 30,000 Union soldiers began moving south into Virginia. They were headed for Manassas, the rail junction that was 26 miles away near a creek called Bull Run.

The location of the much-anticipated first big battle had been previously announced and a parade of spectators followed in the army's wake. Journalists and politicians, their wives and girlfriends, rode out on horseback, gig, buggy, and carriage. They were all well dressed and well provisioned with picnic baskets weighed down by sandwiches, loaves of bread, bottles of wine and champagne, and other delicacies. Armed with parasols to shield them from the summer sun and opera glasses to help them see the carnage more clearly, they were prepared for what was sure to be a most satisfying gladiatorial

*Washington D.C. May 25, 1861*

*To the Father and Mother of Col. Elmer E. Ellsworth:*

*My dear Sir and Madam,*

*In the untimely loss of your noble son, our affliction here, is scarcely less than your own. So much of promised usefulness to one's country, and of bright hopes for one's self and friends, have rarely been so suddenly dashed, as in his fall. In size, in years, and in youthful appearance, a boy only, his power to command men, was surprisingly great. This power, combined with a fine intellect, an indomitable energy, and a taste altogether military, constituted in him, as seemed to me, the best natural talent, in that department, I ever knew.*

*. . .*

*In the hope that it may be no intrusion upon the sacredness of your sorrow, I have ventured to address you this tribute to the memory of my young friend, and your brave and early fallen child.*

*May God give you that consolation which is beyond all earthly power.*

*Sincerely your friend in a common affliction—*

*A Lincoln*

COLONEL BURNSIDE'S BRIGADE, FIRST AND SECOND RHODE ISLAND, AND SEVENTY-FIRST NEW YORK REGIMENTS, WITH THEIR ARTILLERY, ATTACKING THE REBEL BATTERIES AT BULL RUN. SKETCHED ON THE SPOT BY A. WAUD. SEE PAGE 216.

# CITIZENS SHOCKED BY LOST VICTORY AT BULL RUN

## Mrs. Lincoln Refuses To Flee City With Children Insists On Remaining With President

## ULTIMATE VICTORY ASSURED—NATION UNDAUNTED

## REBEL LOSSES ESTIMATED IN THOUSANDS

## President Urged To Use All Means Necessary To Suppress Rebellion

spectacle and thrilling Union victory.

Lincoln, who could hear the artillery, read the telegrams as they came in every 15 minutes from the front. Although they were confusing and conflicting, he was assured of an eventual Northern victory. Relieved, he went for his customary afternoon carriage ride.

But the critical stage of the battle took place while he was on that ride. Not only were federal forces defeated, but many of them were in full retreat, panicking and throwing away anything that might slow them down: hats, coats, backpacks, canteens—even their weapons.

To further complicate the already chaotic scene, they were using the same road that the spectators were now fleeing on. The road was obscured by clouds of dust and clogged by abandoned army wagons and tumbled-over carriages whose wild-eyed horses frantically ran free.

Lincoln watched from his window as the woeful remains of the army returned to the relative safety of the nation's capital. Staggering and sleepwalking, wounded and wrapped in blankets, they fell, exhausted, on the lawns, sidewalks, and steps of houses.

That night, Lincoln listened, silently, to the graphic accounts of the senators and congressmen who had witnessed the battle and its aftermath.

Immediately following the humiliating defeat at Bull Run, President Lincoln put 34-year-old Gen. George McClellan in command of the Army of the Potomac. McClellan had entered West Point when he was only 15 (the age regulations were suspended for him) and, like Lee, graduated second in his class. He had been vice president of the Illinois Central Railroad at the same time Abraham Lincoln was their legal counsel. Handsome, with an erect military bearing, he was charismatic, egotistical in the extreme, and arrogant. He liked to refer to himself as "Young Napoleon."

He worked long hours at his desk drawing up plans and spent 12-hour days in the saddle. Astride his fine mount, his aides in close pursuit, he rode all over the city personally inspecting the camps and overseeing the constant training and drilling of the troops. His positive attitude was transmitted to the men, who liked and respected him. The simulated maneuvers, close-order drills, target practice, and elaborate reviews thrilled the citizens of the city. They were gratified that Washington was no longer vulnerable to Confederate attack.

However, as summer turned into fall, there was still no movement by McClellan's army, no actual fighting the enemy.

According to McClellan, the troops were not quite ready to go on the offensive. Though now 170,000 strong, they were, his intelligence network informed him, vastly outnumbered. He needed more men before he could attack the strongly held Confederate positions.

Lincoln was losing patience.

McClellan resented the president's propensity to drop in and voice his views on military strategy, views the Young Napoleon considered worthless. He spoke of Lincoln disrespectfully in private (calling him an idiot, gorilla, and baboon) and treated him with disdain and, at times, outright rudeness.

One night, Lincoln, his secretary, and Secy. of State Seward dropped in on the general. They were told by his servant that he was expected back from a wedding in an hour. After a while, they asked the servant if McClellan had returned home yet. He had, the servant said, but when informed that the president was waiting, the general had gone straight to bed.

Thereafter, when the president wanted to see McClellan, he called him to the White House.

In the meantime, always slow to dismiss subordinates, Lincoln endured, hoping:

*"I will hold McClellan's horse if he will only bring success."*

The Confederate armies were not attacking the White House, but the president's wife was.

In January, Mary traveled to New York for a two-week clothes-shopping trip. She was keenly aware that the Eastern press and Southern-dominated Washington society viewed her husband as a hick and she worse. Her slave-holding upbringing made her a traitor while her rebel half brothers meant she was a spy. She wanted to show them how fashionably dressed she could be and what a charming and gracious hostess she was. To accomplish that, Mrs. Mary Lincoln needed more than a new wardrobe.

Their new 31-room "home" (the East Room was as large as their entire house in Springfield) was in no condition to be the setting for the type of lavish entertaining that Mary was planning. Entertaining that was not only her due, but essential if her husband was to appear properly presidential despite the war—and, indeed, precisely because of the war. The list of problems was endless: peeling wallpaper, worn carpets, frayed drapes, broken furniture, and rats in the basement.

The shops on Pennsylvania Avenue had improved greatly since she had been there as a congressman's wife but simply couldn't compare with those in nearby Philadelphia and New York. Her trips were a great success, resulting in shipments back to Washington of Bohemian-cut glass, French wallpaper and gold-tasseled drapes, Brussels carpets, Swiss lace curtains, and a selection of the very best in elegant chairs, hassocks, and vases.

Like Gen. McClellan, Mary Lincoln oversaw every detail as she commanded squadrons of workmen who swarmed over the White House. The extensive painting and plastering, along with her equally extensive purchases, turned the Lincoln White House into a glittering jewel.

But it was at a dear, dear price.

Mary had spent much more than her government allocation, a fact that she kept from her husband as long as she could. Her wartime extravagance and her penchant for speaking her mind were to become the subject of constant ridicule, North and South.

*Ink drawing of President and Mrs. Lincoln walking outside the White House*

# 1862

## WILLIE · MCCLELLAN ANTIETAM · EMANCIPATION PROCLAMATION

*A son dies Feb. 20, 1862*

In early February 1862, Mary Lincoln was giving an elaborate ball in the newly decorated White House. The 500 by-invitation-only guests would be served supper (which was being prepared by New York's finest and costliest caterer) at midnight.

Eleven-year-old Willie Lincoln became ill a few days before the ball, and the Lincolns considered canceling. Their doctor, however, assured them that he was not in any serious danger and the glamorous affair took place as scheduled.

A few days later, on February 20, Willie died of bilious fever. Mary collapsed, unable to attend the funeral. She gave away all of his toys, remained in her room for months, canceled all social activities, and never again entered the room where Willie had died or his coffin lay. Eventually she sought out spiritualists, hoping they could, as they promised, help her contact her much-missed son.

Lincoln, who tried to comfort his wife, worried that she was losing her mind. One day, he pointed to the asylum they both could see from the White House and told her: *"Try and control your grief or it will drive you mad, and we may have to send you there."*

Lincoln, although able to "control" his grief, was just as devastated as his wife:

*". . . Did you ever dream of a lost friend, and feel that you were holding sweet communion with that friend, and yet have sad consciousness that it was not a reality? Just so I dream of my boy Willie."*

He had little time for sadness as he resumed his 18-hour workday confronting the ever-increasing list of war-related problems.

George McClellan had transformed the men under his command. Their camps now were properly laid out in the required military fashion, and their food and supplies were distributed effectively. They had become a highly organized, well-trained, and thoroughly drilled army. They remained, however, idle in their winter quarters.

The general hinted at a grand plan that would win the war with one decisive battle, but would reveal no details.

*"He's got the slows,"* Lincoln remarked.

Lincoln was being pressured to remove McClellan from command and replace him with just about anybody. *". . . Anybody will do for you, but I must have somebody,"* was the president's frustrated but characteristically realistic response. Tentative in only his second year in office and perhaps patient to a fault with people, Lincoln failed to reprimand McClellan.

———————

The only good news was coming out of the West. In early February, Ulysses Simpson Grant captured Tennessee's Fort Henry and, ten days later, Fort Donelson. He insisted the Confederates accept his terms of unconditional surrender and took 14,000 prisoners.

Grant attended West Point, but only because his father insisted. He was an excellent horseman, even setting a jumping record (6'6"). Withdrawn, sensitive but unwilling to reveal it, Grant always wore a rumpled uniform, chain-smoked cigars, got a reputation for drinking, and was forced to resign.

In civilian life, he failed at a variety of occupations: bill collecting, real estate, even selling firewood. At one point, he was so poor he pawned a gold watch to buy his family Christmas presents. He ended up unhappily working at his father's harness shop.

Then came the war.

Two months after his success at Forts Henry and Donelson, Grant was taken by surprise near Shiloh Church, a country meetinghouse. The rebels attacked at dawn and Grant's troops were badly deployed. He was nearly defeated by the end of the first day. But he and his men rallied, and on the second,

*Gen. Ulysses S. Grant*

when reinforcements arrived, the Confederate attack was repulsed.

There were rumors and reports that his men had been caught off guard because Grant was drinking again. In Washington, there were calls for his removal. Lincoln refused to listen: *"I can't spare this man; he fights."*

The truth was Grant only drank when he was stationed at remote army outposts where he was bored and missed his family. He never drank when it counted. Grant was a clear-headed, determined soldier who could be ruthless and was always cool under fire.

In the critical Eastern theater of the war, however, Gen. McClellan continued to be cautious in the extreme. He consistently overestimated the enemy's troops strength (aided by the erroneous intelligence reports he eagerly believed) and constantly called for reinforcements.

*"Sending men to that army is like shoveling fleas across the barnyard—not half of them get there. . . . If I gave McClellan all the men he asked for they could not find room to lie down. They'd have to sleep standing up."*

Even when McClellan finally moved the Army of the Potomac south, he failed to attack or, after an encounter, pursue the enemy. He cited an endless list of reasons:

- He couldn't commit fresh troops because he was holding them in reserve.
- His lines of retreat were not properly established.
- The footbridges hadn't been constructed yet.
- The canal boats weren't the right size.
- The maps he was given were faulty.

- His supply trains were inadequate.
- The incessant rain made the roads impassable.

*". . . [McClellan] seemed to think, in defiance of Scripture, that Heaven sent its rain only on the just and not the unjust."*

In March, the Confederate army executed a tactical retreat in order to better defend Richmond. Northern journalists discovered that the Confederate forces were not nearly as large as McClellan had claimed. They also found that the retreating rebels had left behind the menacing cannons that had kept McClellan at bay. On closer inspection, they turned out to be logs painted black and mounted like cannons.

McClellan believed he would win by employing superior strategy at the appropriate time, but that time never came.

McClellan disastrously underestimated the intelligence and capabilities of Robert E. Lee. Tall, stately, graying Lee was now in command of the main Confederate army. He was able, with uncanny precision, to predict McClellan's every move. Along with Gen. Thomas "Stonewall" Jackson (McClellan's classmate at West Point), Lee harassed, outsmarted, and out-generaled the Young Napoleon at every turn.

Unsettled by their audacious tactics, McClellan was unwilling to launch an attack on Richmond. At one point, his army was within four miles of the Confederate capital, so close they could hear the church bells toll.

Exasperated, Lincoln traveled to Virginia to visit the troops and talk to his general face-to-face in the field. The ever-arrogant McClellan presented the president with a lengthy official letter that explained his political philosophy and offered his recommendations for future government policy. (He was already considering running against Lincoln in the 1864 election.)

Lincoln did not respond, but later, when asked how he felt about it, said:

"*. . . It made me think of the man whose horse kicked up and stuck his foot through the stirrup. He said to the horse, 'If you are going to get on I will get off.'*"

Shortly after, Lincoln removed McClellan as general in chief while allowing him to remain in charge of the Army of the Potomac.

Gen. Thomas "Stonewall" Jackson

In late June, Lincoln transferred John Pope from the West and placed him in command of the newly formed Army of Virginia. Pope was disliked by his peers and was even more of a braggart than McClellan. When he arrived, he told the troops that he was accustomed to only seeing the backs of the enemy. In late August,

he was humiliated at the second battle of Bull Run, where casualties were five times higher than the year before.

By September, Union forces were demoralized and beaten down. Lincoln believed they needed to have their confidence restored, something only McClellan could accomplish. With profound doubts and deep misgivings— *"We must use the tools we have"*—the President placed Gen. George McClellan, once again, in command.

Lincoln had come to mistrust the capabilities, views, and recommendations of all Union generals he had come in contact with. They disliked one another, indulged in petty jealousies, communicated badly or not at all, and, like McClellan, promised much but delivered little.

Although he knew he lacked a West Point education and the experience only gotten in the field, Lincoln was thinking of taking over the day-to-day military operations. He began to teach himself the art of war: studying military texts he borrowed from the Library of Congress, reading the battle reports coming in with increased intensity, and conferring more frequently with field officers.

Since the Union defeat at the first battle of Bull Run a year earlier, he had been struggling to develop an effective military strategy for winning the war.

And time, he knew, was running out.

The 11 Confederate States of America were proving to be a formidable foe. They formed a country larger than any in Europe, other than Russia. They were fighting on familiar soil, protecting their homes from an invader. Although invariably outnumbered, they were able to maneuver their troops quickly and effectively.

The North possessed a great manpower

advantage: 20 million people lived in the 22 Northern states while only 5 million whites and 4 million slaves lived in the South. In addition, unlike the rural, agricultural South, the North could produce weapons of war quickly and in great quantity.

*"I state my general idea of this war to be that we have greater numbers, and the enemy has the greater facility of concentrating forces upon points of collision; that we must fail unless we can find some way of making our advantage overmatch his; and that this can be done by menacing him with superior forces at different points, at the same time. . . ."*

Lincoln had steadfastly maintained that the war was being fought solely to preserve the Union. Now he believed that the worsening military situation the North was facing—the possibility of losing the war—called for dire political measures that would have military ramifications.

*"I felt that we . . . must change our tactics or lose the game."*

He was contemplating, for the first time, using his war powers to take steps aimed directly at the South's slave population.

The majority of slaves in the South continued to till the soil, work the fields, and bring in the crops. This allowed a high percentage of the white population to fight. In addition, the Confederate military used slaves to load and unload supplies, repair and build bridges and tunnels, construct fortifications, dig trenches, wash and mend uniforms, and cook and serve food.

The people in the North had become weary of the war. The enthusiasm and patriotism of 1861 had waned. Reduced enlistments and reenlistments, increasing desertion rates, and the incredibly high number of casualties were

*March 1862: The false cannons abandoned by Confederate defenders. First discovered by reporters, they are being examined by Union troops.*

depleting Union ranks. Free blacks living in the North and slaves escaping from the South could help fill those ranks.

*"I shall do nothing in malice. What I deal with is too vast for malicious dealing. Still I must save this government if possible. What I cannot do, of course, I will not do; but it may as well be understood, once and for all, that I shall not surrender this game leaving any available card unplayed."*

Working at a desk in the cipher room of the War Department's telegraph office (where he could escape the unceasing pressure of the White House), Lincoln began to draft a presidential order abolishing slavery in the states that had seceded from the Union. Slavery in the loyal border states of Maryland, Kentucky, Delaware, and Missouri would be unaffected.

This Emancipation Proclamation would, Lincoln believed, profoundly change the nature and objectives of the Civil War. The war would now be fought not only to preserve the Union but to change it to one in which slavery no longer existed.

*"This government cannot much longer play a game in which it stakes all, and its enemies stake nothing. Those enemies must understand that they cannot experiment for ten years to destroy the government, and if they fail come back to the Union unhurt."*

Members of Lincoln's Cabinet, fellow Republicans, abolitionists, black leaders like escaped slave Frederick Douglass, and others had advocated making the war about slavery from the beginning. Lincoln, fearing such a radical position, resisted, until now.

He presented a preliminary draft to his stunned Cabinet. Secy. of State Seward strongly believed that an announcement this momentous must not be perceived by the populace as a desperate act coming from an administration fearing they were losing the

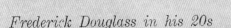
*Frederick Douglass in his 20s*

war. It should only be issued, Seward urged, after a Union military victory.

Lincoln agreed and kept the preliminary draft locked in a desk drawer in the telegraph office, revising it from time to time, and waiting.

Abraham Lincoln agonized about destiny, God's will, and the Civil War that was destroying the country.

*"In great contests each party claims to act in accordance with the will of God. Both may be, and one must be, wrong. God cannot be for and against the same thing at the same time. In the present civil war it is quite possible that God's purpose is something different from the purpose of either party; . . . I am almost ready to say that . . . God wills this contest, and wills that it shall not end yet . . . he could have either saved or destroyed the Union without human contest. Yet the contest*

1862

*began. And having begun, he could give the final victory to either side any day. Yet the contest proceeds."*

Lincoln was unsure if God was on the Union side. He would look for a sign. A Union victory would be that sign, as would its absence.

———

Confederate Gen. Robert E. Lee was looking for a victory as fervently as President Lincoln. Now that he had forced federal troops out of Virginia, he could turn his attention to attacking on Union soil for the first time in the war. His army was sighted in early September crossing the upper Potomac, heading north. Union military intelligence was unable to predict their intention or destination, but

their movements undoubtedly threatened Washington and Baltimore. There were even rumors that Philadelphia, New York, and Boston might be in danger.

On September 13, a Union soldier discovered an envelope that had probably fallen out of a careless Confederate courier's pouch. The envelope contained three cigars with a paper wrapped around them. The paper was covered on both sides with official-looking writing that outlined, in detail, Lee's unconventional plan to split up his army.

McClellan's troops outnumbered Lee's by two to one, and his artillery support was superior. Now, he knew precisely where to strike Lee's weakened, divided army.

*President Lincoln working at the War Department's Telegraph Office*

Inexplicably, he failed to take advantage of this miraculous discovery, allowing critical hours to pass before making any decision. Even then, he acted cautiously.

Lee's offensive posture made engagement unavoidable. The two armies met just 52 miles from Washington, near Antietam Creek in Maryland. The battle began in the early morning hours of September 17. When the fighting ended that night, 23,000 men lay dead; it was the bloodiest single day of the war.

McClellan wired Lincoln that he was fighting the greatest battle in all of military history and victory was complete. Lincoln once again erroneously assumed that Lee's Confederate army had been destroyed. They might have been if McClellan had deployed the 25,000 fresh troops he had in reserve, but he didn't.

Lee left the field of battle with his fighting force intact. They had, however, suffered terrible losses—one out of every four men, gone. His hopes for an invasion of the North, attacking the Union capital and ending the war, were gone. Lee had been forced to retreat back to the safety of the South.

---

Antietam was a tactical Union victory and the sign that Abraham Lincoln was looking for.

On September 22, 1862, five days after the bloodbath at Antietam, President Lincoln issued the Emancipation Proclamation:

*". . . on the first day of January in the year of our Lord one thousand eight hundred and sixty three, all persons held as slaves within any state, or designated part of a state, the people whereof shall then be in rebellion against the United States, shall be then, thenceforward and forever free. . . ."*

Lincoln's startling announcement predictably provoked a variety of emotional reactions. Abolitionists and Radical Republicans rejoiced, their efforts vindicated. The president had finally elevated the war to a higher moral ground. The North would now have a renewed sense of purpose.

Others in the North disagreed. Lincoln had succumbed, they believed, to pressure from these radicals and revolutionaries. He had gone too far. The Emancipation Proclamation would only serve to divide the North and unite the South.

White Southerners believed that Lincoln knew he couldn't beat them in a fair fight, so he was freeing their slaves. It confirmed their suspicions that Lincoln and the people living in the North were intent upon destroying their entire way of life.

# ANTIETAM

## DREADFUL CARNAGE

### Greatest Battle Of War

### Rebel Army In Full Retreat
### Leave Behind Dead And Wounded
### Thousands Taken Prisoner

### Complete Victory Wires McClellan

1862

In October, Lincoln visited McClellan near Antietam, hoping to persuade him to move south and engage Lee's army.

Early one morning, the president and an Illinois friend were walking around the sprawling camp, stopping on a hill that overlooked row after row of soldiers' tents. Lincoln asked his companion if he knew what *"all this"* was. His friend offered that it was the Army of the Potomac. *"No,"* Lincoln said. *"This is General McClellan's bodyguard."*

Back in Washington, Lincoln grew even

*President Lincoln visiting Gen. McClellan's headquarters after Antietam. McClellan is sixth from the left.*

more frustrated as McClellan had still not made a move against Lee. "Little Mac" cited, instead, his usual lengthy list of excuses.

Lincoln wired back:

*"I have just read your dispatch about sore tongued and fatigued horses. Will you pardon me for asking what the horses of*

*your army have done since the battle of Antietam to fatigue anything?"*

Lincoln had to finally face the fact that McClellan was capable of organizing, training, and preparing an army but not commanding one on the battlefield. He lacked the aggressive, offensive instincts that were the fundamental characteristics of a superior general. He had, over the past year, become completely unnerved by Lee's and Jackson's skill and daring.

Some believed worse of McClellan.

Although always professing to be loyal to the Union, his pro-slavery, anti-black views were well known. His critics claimed that he did not attack the rebels because he didn't want to do anything that would bring about freedom for the slaves. He wanted the war to end now, peaceably, with the seceding Southern states returning to a new union with him, Young Napoleon, as dictator.

On November 5, Lincoln removed George McClellan from command.

Addressing Congress in December, Lincoln said:

*"The dogmas of the quiet past are inadequate to the stormy present. The occasion is piled high with difficulty, and we must rise with the occasion. As our case is new, so we must think anew, and act anew . . . then we shall save our country.*

*". . . We cannot escape history. . . . The fiery trial through which we pass will light us down, in honor or dishonor, to the latest generation . . . in giving freedom to the slave, we assure freedom to the free— honorable alike in what we give, and what we preserve. We shall nobly save, or meanly lose, the last best hope of earth."*

# MAGNIFICENT T:
# FOUGHT ON NORTHERI

## SPECTACULAR ARTILLERY DUEL

### Rebels Repulsed By Valiant Union Soldiers
### Horrific Slaughter During Desperate, Failed Charge

## REBELS SUFFER FEARFUL LOSSES

### Lee's Entire Army Whipped And In Full Retreat

### Special Dispatch To National News: High-Ranking
### Confederate Officers Believed Killed

### On To Richmond! Is The Cry

# 1863

**CHANCELLORSVILLE
GETTYSBURG · GRANT
VICKSBURG · 54TH MASS.**

**BLACK SOLDIERS
"FOUR SCORE . . ."
MARY AND THE BOYS**

*Confederate Prisoners of War*

# REE DAY BATTLE
# OIL RESULTS DECISIVE

In the winter and spring of 1863, the president continued to search fruitlessly for a general who could lead the men, fight the enemy, and win the war. Over a 12-month period, Lincoln placed five different generals in command of the Union army. Some, like McClellan, were unwilling to attack; others proved uncertain and confused, while Lee and his generals continued to act confidently, intelligently, and decisively.

At Chancellorsville, Virginia, in late April, Lee audaciously divided his army three times when confronted, yet again, by superior numbers. It was yet another disgraceful defeat for the Union army, whose general seemed bewildered and who later resigned.

*"My God! My God! What will the country say!"* Lincoln cried.

But Lee's brilliant victory at Chancellorsville was costly. Stonewall Jackson, returning from a night reconnaissance mission, was mistaken for the enemy and shot by his own men. His amputated left arm became infected, and he died of pneumonia eight days later.

Despite the loss of his most trusted general, Robert E. Lee believed that the time to invade the North and win the war was now. By late June, he was in Maryland, moving into Pennsylvania, seizing much-needed food and supplies along the way.

---

On July 1, two Union cavalry brigades collided with a Confederate infantry brigade at Gettysburg, a small town 75 miles north of Washington, where a number of roads converged. What began as a skirmish rapidly escalated into a full-scale, three-day battle.

Union Gen. George Meade was, thanks to his temper and looks, known as the "Old Snapping Turtle." He had been in command of his 85,000 men for only a few days (the previous general having asked to be relieved of command in late June). Lee wanted to attack quickly, hoping to overcome the federal forces before their entire army arrived at the scene of battle. His cavalry, who usually provided him with accurate information of the enemy's whereabouts, failed him, and he was forced to deploy his 65,000 men blindly.

On the second day, Lee met with Gen. Longstreet, who was now, with Jackson gone, his best general (and, in this war of Americans versus Americans, the best man at Grant's wedding). Lee wanted Longstreet to attack the Union's left flank. Longstreet, who strongly disagreed with the strategy, was slow to make the attack, arriving and deploying his men late that afternoon.

At one point, Union soldiers commanded by Col. Joshua Chamberlain, a former minister and professor who had already been wounded twice, fought off wave after wave of desperate rebel attacks. A third of Chamberlain's men were dead or wounded and the rest were ex-

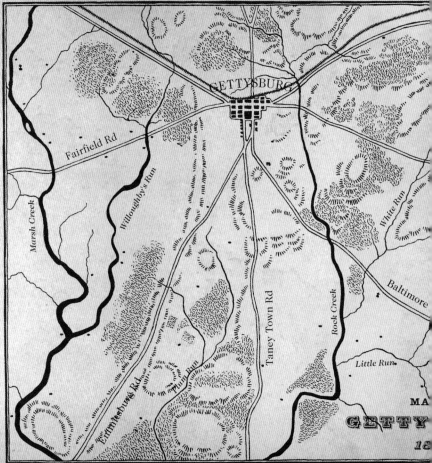

hausted and running out of ammunition. Chamberlain ordered a rarely executed bayonet counterattack. His startled but obedient troops surprised the rebels and captured hundreds of prisoners, continuing to hold their critical position. Elsewhere, Union soldiers fought with equal valor.

---

At the end of day two, Gen. Lee believed that one more attack would do it. He needed a decisive victory and he needed it now, here. The South needed it. His men, who revered him, would do anything he asked of them. Lee assumed the Union center was vulnerable, having reinforced their flanks during day two. He would attack there.

The Union artillery opened up at dawn, and the Confederate artillery responded. But the rebels were short of guns and ammunition, and the artillery was ineffective, seriously lessening the charge's chance of success.

Standing shoulder to shoulder a mile across, the 15,000 rebel soldiers advanced across the open field, under constant artillery fire,

closing ranks as their comrades fell all around them. Some made it over the fences and past the trenches, but only a handful got over the stone wall, where they were immediately killed or captured by the entrenched Union infantry.

Lee and his army disappeared during the rain-soaked night, taking 10,000 injured men with them and leaving 7,000 wounded behind.

Nearly 50,000 men and boys were killed, wounded, missing in action, or taken prisoner in the three-day battle. One man watched his own son get killed.

Mary Virginia Wade was a civilian casualty. "Jennie," as she was known by most, had turned 20 the month before. She was engaged to a corporal in the Union army who was fighting somewhere in Virginia.

On the first day, she went to help her sister who was bedridden, having just given birth. Her 12-year-old brother had already

Today, they are buried near each other at Gettysburg.

The Army of the Potomac had forced Robert E. Lee to retreat and abandon his plans to invade the North, at least for now. The Union had won the battle, but by not pursuing Lee—yet again—they had failed to win the war.

been arrested by the rebels for refusing to give them the family horse.

Loyal to the North and fearless, Jennie Wade gave Union soldiers water to fill their empty canteens and bread to fill their empty stomachs. On July 3, she rose at dawn and started making the bread. At 8:00 AM, a rebel bullet went through the kitchen door and her heart, killing her instantly.

Her fiancé had been wounded two weeks earlier and died of his wounds nine days after Jennie. Neither knew of the tragic fate of the other.

*Jennie Wade*

*Union dead after the Battle of Gettysburg*

Only Ulysses S. Grant was proving to be as daring as Robert E. Lee.

In early May, he wired the president that there might not be any word from him; and for weeks, there wasn't. Lincoln followed his progress by reading confiscated Southern newspapers and intercepted Confederate-coded flag signals.

Wearing the same shirt, carrying only a toothbrush, asking for no reinforcements, purposely breaking off from his supply base, and living off the land, Grant led his men relentlessly forward. When he emerged, they had won five engagements, captured Jackson, Mississippi, and had tried repeatedly to take Vicksburg, Mississippi, located strategically on the Mississippi River, but were repulsed.

Grant laid siege to the city, cutting it off entirely from the outside world. The civilians who remained lived in caves, some driven insane by the round-the-clock shelling. Most were ill, reduced to eating cats, dogs, horses, and mules to avoid starvation.

On July 4, after holding out for 48 days, the rebel garrison at Vicksburg surrendered to Grant, who took 31,000 prisoners. (All were released after promising not to rejoin the fight.)

---

The nearly simultaneous victories in the Eastern theater of the war at Gettysburg and in the West at Vicksburg boosted Northern morale greatly. What had been put in motion at Antietam continued. The tide was turning. Slowly, too slowly. Painfully, too painfully. But it was turning. The South was, if not yet losing the war, unable to win it.

---

President Lincoln was also facing serious trouble on the civilian front. In the Northern states, there was widespread heated opposition to the new draft law and the idea of enlisting emancipated slaves and free blacks as soldiers.

The draft law allowed a draftee to hire a substitute for 300 dollars. In the eyes of many, this gave an unfair advantage to the rich. Two weeks after Gettysburg and Vicksburg, rioting erupted in New York City. Angered by the draft law and competition from blacks for hard-to-find jobs, mobs of Irish working men went on a four-day rampage. They roamed the streets, breaking into and looting stores, burning draft offices, setting fire to the Colored Orphan Asylum, brutally murdering black residents, and terrorizing the city.

Federal soldiers, some returning from fighting at Gettysburg, finally restored order— but not before 105 people, mostly black, were killed.

Lincoln had resisted using blacks as soldiers. But, as the war dragged on, he knew he needed men, lots of men.

*"The colored population is the great available and yet unavailed of, force for restoring the Union,"* he said.

The Emancipation Proclamation, which was announced, as promised, on January 1, 1863, prepared the way for the enlistment of black soldiers in the Union army.

Some believed that blacks would never fight—that they would run away or be captured without firing a shot. Others thought they would return to their plantations and

*Lewis Douglass at 23*

*Charles Douglass at 19*

massacre their former masters. Some Union soldiers and officers said that they would rather desert than fight with black soldiers, and did.

Some slaves remained loyal to their masters, reluctant to leave the place where they were born or had lived most of their lives. Some feared these strange Yankee invaders. But many others rejoiced when liberated by the Union armies, left their masters and their plantations, and fled north, enlisting at the earliest opportunity.

Frederick Douglass was himself an escaped slave. An eloquent and forceful speaker, he had become an outspoken abolitionist and the most prominent black man in America. Now, in March 1863, actively recruiting blacks for the army, he was concerned that they were being used only as laborers, not soldiers, or were serving in segregated outfits under white officers and receiving less pay than white soldiers.

The president invited him to the White House—itself a revolutionary act—and assured him that, in time, that would change. Douglass, who admired Lincoln, took him at his word. His two sons had enlisted in the Fifty-fourth Massachusetts Infantry (Colored)—the first full regiment of black soldiers.

The Fifty-fourth was commanded by boyish, blond, blue-eyed Robert Gould Shaw, the son of wealthy New England abolitionist parents. He had seen action at Cedar Mountain and Antietam and had accepted as his duty the command of the Fifty-fourth.

The day after the New York draft riots ended, Col. Shaw and his men were hundreds of miles south in South Carolina. Under Shaw's firm hand they were disciplined, well trained, and had already seen action.

Col. Shaw had accepted the honor of leading the assault on the well-defended, nearly impregnable Confederate position at Fort Wagner, which guarded the mouth of Charleston Harbor.

Assembling his men for the assault, Shaw told them that the whole world would be watching. Dismounting and leading from the front (despite a premonition of death), he led his men across the strip of sand, through the seawater, moats, pits, and sharpened stakes, and up the sheer sand walls of the fort as hand grenades and rifle fire rained down on them.

He ordered them to halt, lie down in the sand, fix bayonets, and charge. A handful made it to the top before Shaw was shot in the chest and, waving his men forward with his sword, fell dead. Inside the fort, the men of the Fifty-fourth engaged in hand-to-hand combat with the rebels but were forced back.

One-third of the officers and half of the men of Col. Shaw's brigade were killed or wounded during the assault. His body was thrown into a ditch along with his men's. Notified by the Confederates of this presumably ignominious burial place, Col. Shaw's father insisted that his son's body remain where it was.

The fort finally fell on September 6, with the men of the Fifty-fourth participating in the siege that brought it down.

The heroic assault on Fort Wagner proved that black troops were as capable of fighting courageously as white soldiers; it showed that they too were willing to die for their country.

Seventy-five percent of those black Americans eligible to enlist did. Eventually 180,000—many emancipated slaves—served in the Union army. Of that number, 34,000 gave up their lives.

President Lincoln turned down nearly all invitations to speak—he simply had no time. In November 1863, however, he was asked to make some appropriate remarks at the dedication of the cemetery at Gettysburg. Thousands of men who had died there were unidentified and/or hastily buried in shallow graves. They were to be properly laid to rest.

Lincoln accepted, believing it was an opportunity to say something about the true meaning of the war.

While the opening speaker delivered his two-hour oration, Lincoln looked over the battlefield. The trees cut in half by artillery; the coffins scattered about; the decaying carcasses of the dead army horses; and the souvenir hunters combing the field for bullets and shell fragments.

After being introduced by his friend Ward Lamon, Lincoln rose, put on his steel-bowed glasses, took a folded paper out of his coat pocket and, only glancing at it from time to time, began to speak:

*"Four score and seven years ago . . ."*

———————————

When Lincoln returned from Gettysburg, he was confined to bed with a mild case of smallpox. Working propped up on pillows, he saw few visitors. Referring to the constant requests for jobs and favors, he said: *"I now have something I can give everybody."* There was no denying the president's dismal state of mind:

*"Rest, I don't know about . . . it. I suppose it is good for the body. But the tired part of me is inside and out of reach."*

Over the summer, Mary had been injured in a carriage accident. The seat had become unbolted—someone trying to harm her husband, presumably. The driver was thrown, the horse panicked, and Mary hurt her head badly when she too was thrown to the ground. The wound became infected, and she remained in bed for weeks and had not yet fully recovered.

Still dressed in mourning, she attended séances conducted at the White House, saying that Willie came to see her in the night.

There were rumors that Mary Lincoln was a spy because her half brothers were in the rebel army. She was, therefore, suspected of providing the enemy with information that only she had access to. Mary Lincoln received so much hate mail that all letters had to be screened by a secretary. She was tense and nervous and had a frightened, fearful look about her.

She continued to enjoy her shopping trips to New York, Boston, and Philadelphia, and vacations in New England. She spent time visiting the wounded boys in the Washington hospitals. Her friendship with Elizabeth Keckly, a slave who had raised money to buy her freedom, was gratifying, as well. It was because of her that Mary worked to raise money for emancipated slaves who had come north and were now in need of food and clothing.

———————————

Lincoln's relationship with his wife, once a welcome source of intellectual companionship and professional support, had, sadly, deteriorated over time—especially during the years of his presidency. Robert was away, studying at Harvard. Distant as a child, he had grown to be an aloof young man (folks said he was a Todd, not a Lincoln).

The president tried to spend as much time with his two little codgers as the pressing duties of his office allowed. The two boys were very different. Willie had been gentle, affectionate, handsome, and studious. He liked nothing better than to spend his time alone: reading, writing, and working on his history scrapbook— much like his father when he was that age.

Tad, with his fragile health, proved to be slow to learn (even when he was ten he couldn't read or dress himself), but that only made his father love him more. Unlike his well-behaved older brother, Tad was impulsive, impudent, and an inveterate troublemaker.

He was quite capable of throwing an impressive temper tantrum when he didn't get his way. Sometimes, his father had to hold him at arm's length while the little boy kicked and screamed.

Both boys liked to go with Lincoln when he visited the armies in the field. They watched while the soldiers drilled and marched. They rode behind Lincoln, tipping their hats just as he did.

Having them running around the White House made it seem so much more like a home than it really was. They would play soldier with the neighborhood boys, go on rooftop reconnaissance missions, reenact battles on the lawn, and parade down the corridors— horns blaring and drums banging.

And, of course, there had been Jack's court-martial.

Jack, their doll, had been discovered asleep on guard duty and sentenced to be executed. The White House gardener, hearing about the planned burial and fearing for his roses, suggested they talk to their father first. Lincoln sagely sized up the situation, took out his executive stationery, and wrote: "The Doll Jack is pardoned by order of the President, A. Lincoln." (A week later Jack was found hung from the bushes. He was, an unrepentant Tad said, a traitor and a spy.)

Now, with Willie gone, Lincoln turned to his mischievous, uninhibited youngest son. Tad's bottomless bag of pranks provided the beleaguered president with the only momentary relief he would find in the world of pain he inhabited.

There was the time Tad ate all the strawberries intended for a state dinner, and another when he snuck up to the attic and pulled simultaneously on all the bell ropes that called the servants.

When visitors arrived at the nearly always-open Lincoln White House, Tad inquired why they wanted to see his father. Then he collected a nickel entrance fee for the privilege. When one visitor came to plead her husband's case, Tad listened sympathetically and then spoke to the president on her behalf.

Sometimes, Tad would use the secret telegraphic knocking code that only he and his father knew to gain entry to the president's office. Other times, he would simply burst in during a Cabinet meeting and point his toy cannon at the speechless (for the moment) Cabinet members.

People said Lincoln was too permissive when it came to both his sons, but especially Tad. They pointed to the time Tad was sick and he refused to take his medicine from anyone. Although he was in a conference, the president came at once when told the nature of the summons. Later, the nurse found a note that promised five dollars to Tad when he was well (he had taken his medicine) and signed "A. Lincoln."

In August, Tad and Mary would escape the summer heat by heading north to Vermont. The president dearly missed his son and sometimes worried about him. When the boy was in Philadelphia with his mother a month before the battle at Gettysburg, Lincoln had a nightmare about Tad's toy gun. The nightmare was so real that he wired Mary to have the gun put somewhere Tad couldn't get it. When he returned from these trips, Tad would fling himself into his father's lap and hug him. They were chums.

Sometimes, Lincoln would take a book, open it, and place it on his knee. Tad would stand next to him while his father explained the pictures and the story.

Late at night, Tad, exhausted from another day of mischief, would finally fall asleep on the leather couch in his father's office. The president, exhausted himself, would finish what he was working on. He would cradle his son in his still-strong frontiersman's arms and carry Tad up to his bedroom.

*The president and his son Tad, February 9, 1864*

1864

# 1864

## GRANT & LEE
## WILDERNESS
## SPOTSYLVANIA · COLD
## HARBOR · PETERSBURG
## SHERMAN · ATLANTA
## REELECTION
## "TOTAL WAR" · THREATS

In March, President Lincoln named Ulysses S. Grant General in Chief of all Union armies: 750,000 men. His brilliant but volatile subordinate, William Tecumseh Sherman (named, most appropriately, after a powerful Shawnee Indian chieftain), took over the army in the West.

*"Grant is the first general I have had. . . . All the rest . . . they wanted me to be the general. I am glad to find a man who can go ahead without me."*

Dressed as usual in his filthy field uniform and accompanied by his teenage son, the unassuming Grant quietly checked into Willard's Hotel. He and Lincoln met for the first time that evening at the weekly White House reception. Word had spread that the new conquering hero might be there. So many people wanted to get a look at him that the diminutive Grant had to stand on a sofa to satisfy them.

The president and his new general in chief agreed upon a war plan that called for simultaneous movements on all fronts—the strategy Lincoln had advocated since McClellan. Grant would attempt to destroy Lee's army in the East, while the eccentric Sherman (he didn't wear boots and wore only one spur) would go after the rebel forces in the West.

In anticipation, Lincoln had called for 500,000 more men in February, and now, in March, 200,000 more.

In early May, the coordinated offensive began.

Grant's first encounter with Lee was in the Wilderness, a trackless, thickly wooded jungle-like area in Virginia. Lee, who was outnumbered two to one, wanted to fight there as the terrain negated Grant's manpower and artillery advantage.

The two-day battle, much of it fought at close quarters, was intense and chaotic.

*Gen. Grant (leaning over Gen. Meade) planning Cold Harbor*

The forest growth was so thick that the men couldn't see one another and lost their way. Their officers were unable to control their movements properly, and at times, the men fired blindly when they heard sounds. At one point, exploding artillery shells set the thick underbrush on fire. Wounded horses and men burned to death where they had fallen, as those who fought on listened helplessly to their anguished cries.

The two armies met again 12 miles away at Spotsylvania Courthouse. During several days of frenzied fighting, 18,000 Union and nearly 12,000 Confederate soldiers were killed or wounded, many in vicious hand-to-hand combat. Lee had tried to personally lead an attack, but his men shouted out that their much-loved general must return to the safety of the rear.

The two armies skirmished every day until early June, when they met at a crossroads called Cold Harbor (the tavern near there didn't serve hot meals). For three days, Grant attacked Lee's lines. Frustrated, he ordered a senseless charge against Lee's well-fortified defensive position. Some of the Union men wrote their names on slips of paper that they pinned to their clothes so they could be properly identified. One man prophetically wrote in his diary that he would be killed that day.

There were 7,000 Union casualties in only 30 minutes.

In mid-June, Grant unsuccessfully assaulted the well-defended, heavily fortified city of Petersburg, Virginia. A Pennsylvania regiment, made up mostly of coal miners, designed a ventilation system that the rebels wouldn't be able to see and dug a 500-foot tunnel under their lines. They filled it with four tons of gunpowder.

The explosion went off as planned, blowing to bits hundreds of Confederate soldiers as the rest ran for their lives. The pursuit, commanded by the incompetent former Army of the Potomac Gen. Burnside, was a tragic fiasco. His division commander was drunk; the rebels recovered, regrouped, and fired on the confused Union soldiers who had become trapped inside their own crater.

Grant notified the president that he would fight it out in Virginia if it took all summer—and it did.

He refused to retreat, unlike all previous Union generals. *"He didn't scare worth a damn,"* as his men, who were inspired by his aggressive posture, put it.

He attacked Lee wherever and whenever he found him. The battles over the previous three years, although horrific, had been sporadic. Now, the fighting was relentless. When the men weren't fighting, they were marching, digging entrenchments, or recuperating from mental and physical exhaustion.

Grant was driving Lee south, toward Richmond, but at a terrible cost. The Union lost more than 64,000 men that spring and summer. But Lee was losing men too, men he couldn't replace.

Injured soldiers—many gravely injured—were being brought back to the nation's capital

*Armory Square Hospital, Washington, D.C.*

1864

in what seemed like an endless procession. There were, by now, more than 20 military hospitals set up in churches, government, and other public buildings in Washington.

---

One night, Lincoln stopped his carriage as a line of the wounded went past:

*"Look . . . at those poor fellows. I cannot bear it. This suffering, this loss of life is dreadful."*

Each day, newspapers listed the dead. Each day, parents and loved ones read letters from those still alive describing the slaughter that was swirling around them.

People began calling Grant a "butcher" and demanded that Lincoln, whom they blamed, replace him. Northern morale, which had peaked in March with Grant's arrival in Washington, sank to a new low that summer. The Northern states were weary of the war and saw no end to it.

---

Robert E. Lee was determined to relieve the pressure Grant was exerting on Petersburg and Richmond. To accomplish this, Lee conceived a typically brilliant and bold countermove.

Confederate Gen. Jubal Early was ordered to take 15,000 men, head north, threaten Baltimore, and attack Washington, if possible. Lee hoped that Early's mission would force Grant to divert troops from Virginia. A daring raid on Washington might also do further damage to the North's sagging civilian morale.

Early's troops, traveling light and fast, went undetected at first, and on July 5, they crossed the Potomac into Maryland. They tore up train tracks, burned down houses, and threatened two towns with destruction

if a hefty ransom wasn't paid. This was in retaliation for the destruction Union troops had brought to the South. Both towns paid.

Residents of Maryland, Pennsylvania, and New York, aware that most of the Union army was fighting in Virginia, became alarmed. Refugees from the countryside clogged the roads leading to the presumed safety of the capital and, upon arrival, reported that there were rebels everywhere. The War Deptartment, fearing that the citizens of Washington would panic, had censored news of Early's movements. On July 9, the rebels defeated Union forces and headed for Washington, cutting all telegraph lines along the way.

In the now-panicked capital, new recruits,

---

**Report of killed, wounded and missing of the 102d regiment since May 25, 1864.**

Killed.
Archibald Henderson, Co E.
David L Crosby, Co B.
Adam Y Stokes, Co B.

Wounded.
D Cunningham, A-stomach.
E M Henton, A-hand & arm.
George Golden, A-hand.
Sgt S D James, C-head.
Charles Reilly, C-arm.
Densil M Gould, D-leg.
Wm Moran, E-arm.
Sgt M Whitbeck, G-head.
1st Sgt D Shannon, I-head.
Corp R Downs, I-hand.
Enos Chapin, I-arm.
John Hopkins, I-side.
Corp Edwd Lyons, I-hand.
1st Sgt J Richardson, K-arm.
Corp Geo Barrison, K-leg.
J Browm, K-leg amput'd.

Missing.
1st Sgt W H Nevins, G-since May 25 '64.
L Smith, B-since May 28, '64.
John Colwell, A-since May 25, '64.

Killed, 3; wounded, 16; missing, 3. Total, 22.

government clerks, and wounded soldiers in the hospital who could walk were issued rifles and hastily deployed to defend the city from attack. Without the president's knowledge, a Navy warship was stationed at the docks, should he and his family have to be evacuated. When Lincoln found out about this, he was greatly displeased.

On July 11, Early's troops approached Fort Stevens, one of more than 50 forts surrounding Washington, which was only five miles away. President Lincoln rode out to the fort and, on two separate occasions, mounted a parapet and looked out at the skirmishing through borrowed field glasses. His 6'4" frame and eight-inch stovepipe hat presented rebel sharp-shooters with a tempting target. Both times, soldiers told him firmly to get down, and once, a surgeon standing next to him was wounded in the leg. This was the first time an American president personally faced enemy fire.

Grant's reinforcements arrived just in time, and Early was forced to retreat. The reinforcements, however, were not enough to affect Grant's ongoing Virginia offensive.

That same month, President Lincoln called for 500,000 more men.

═══════════════

Fifty-five-year-old Abraham Lincoln had his own battle looming on the horizon: the November 1864 presidential election. He refused to postpone or cancel it, as some suggested:

*"We can not have a free government without elections and if the rebellion could force us to forgo, or postpone a nation's election, it might fairly claim to have already conquered and ruined us."*

By the summer of 1864, Lincoln was one of the most unpopular presidents in the nation's 90-year history. No president had been reelected to a second term in over 32 years. Added to this was the opposition within his own party: Moderates thought he was too radical, and radicals too moderate. His own secretary of the treasury was conspiring to

*Union supply wagons filled with provisions for Gen. Grant's troops pass through Petersburg, Virginia.*

run against him, and Grant was being talked about as a possible candidate (Grant refused to have anything to do with it). Lincoln said:

*I wish they would stop thrusting that subject of the Presidency into my face. I don't want to hear anything about it.*

But the truth was he had decided to run.

The election would show whether or not the people in the North believed in union and emancipation for the slaves, whether the past three years had been in vain. He believed he was the only one who could bring the nation safely through to the end of this terrible war.

He had considered discussing peace terms with the Confederate States of America, as some had urged. He even considered leaving the question of slavery open, but could not bring himself to betray the black Americans who were fighting for the Union army:

*"If they stake their lives for us they must be prompted by the strongest motive—even the promise of freedom. And the promise, being made, must be kept."*

Confederate President Jefferson Davis would accept only complete independence and the continuation of slavery. Lincoln could not accept anything less than the preservation of the Union and the abolishment of slavery.

The war would go on.

Lincoln was, in the end, unanimously nominated by his party. The Democrats nominated George McClellan and promised peace immediately upon his election. They accused Lincoln of advocating race mixing, and Lincoln's party accused the Democrats of being traitors. It was an ugly campaign.

News from the battlefield would decide the election.

Gen. William T. Sherman

On September 1, after two and a half months of battles and maneuvers, Sherman's troops finally captured Atlanta, Georgia. The city was not only a strategically important rail junction and manufacturing center, but a symbol of Southern rebellion second in importance only to Richmond.

That same month, Gen. Phillip Sheridan's cavalry was dutifully following Grant's orders. Virginia's Shenandoah Valley had been used by Lee's army as a source of food and an avenue north throughout the war. Grant wanted that to end. He told Sheridan to make the land so barren that a crow flying across the valley would have to bring its own food—when Sheridan was finished it would.

Sherman's and Sheridan's relentless and successful tactics, overseen by Grant, assured Lincoln's reelection on November 8: Winning 212 to 21 in electoral votes and 55 percent of the popular vote. Perhaps most gratifying to the president was his overwhelming majority of the soldiers' vote.

at a variety of civilian occupations: banking, real estate, the law. He was, before war came, a superintendent at a southern military academy. Nervous, overly sensitive, depressed at times, and nearly insane other times, he was also highly intelligent, honest, and perceptive.

Sherman was one of the very few who believed from the outset that the war would be a long and bloody one and that people had no idea how terrible it was going to be. He no longer considered it a war between armies but between peoples. The hostile Southern population had to suffer first-

President Lincoln, in concert with Grant and supported by Sherman and Sheridan, began to wage war with increased intensity and ferocity. He and his generals now believed that "total war" was the only way to achieve victory. A war attacking not only the enemy's armies but their economy and the lives of their civilians. It was a strategy aimed at destroying the Confederacy's ability and will to continue the war.

Sherman attended West Point, where he earned a considerable number of demerits. Like his good friend Grant, he failed

*Atlanta: A Confederate weapons and ammunition train purposely blown up by retreating rebels*

hand the horrors of war if it was ever to end.

He urged Lincoln and Grant to let him take his 62,000-man veteran army and march from Atlanta to Georgia's Atlantic coast, destroying everything in its path.

Lincoln and Grant agreed to Sherman's audacious and dangerous plan.

By mid-November, after two and a half months of occupying Atlanta, Sherman had evacuated most of the civilian population. Now he set fire to everything of military value, the flames spreading until one-third of the city was on fire. The fires burned so brightly that at night, soldiers a mile away could read letters from home.

Sherman stood on a hill with his men and watched the smoldering ruins of Atlanta. The black smoke hung over the city. A passing band played "The Battle Hymn of the Republic," and the men began to sing:

*Glory, glory hallelujah*
*Glory, glory hallelujah*
*His truth is marching on.*

Sherman and his men marched on. They would travel light. Each man carried a blanket rolled up in his rubber poncho, a backpack, a 20-day supply of hardtack and coffee, a tin cup, weapons, and 40 rounds of small-arms ammunition (the rest was in the wagons). Sherman carried maps, whiskey, cigars, and a change of underwear. Their 25-mile-long supply train included 64 artillery guns drawn by eight-horse teams, 600 ambulances, wagons carrying pontoon bridges, and a herd of 10,000 cattle.

Sherman had cut himself off from all rail support, any potential reinforcement, and all lines of communication with the North, where they began to call his men the "lost army."

For three weeks, Lincoln heard nothing.

*"I know what hole he went in at, but I can't tell what hole he will come out of."*

They moved through hostile territory in two columns, spread at times 30–60 miles apart and traveling only ten miles a day to ensure maximum damage. They destroyed factories, warehouses, water towers, rail depots, and ripped up railroad tracks. The ties were burned in the bonfires they lit, and the rails heated and twisted around trees so that they could never be used again. They were called "Sherman neckties."

They burned crops and farms; took, ate, ran off, or killed livestock; destroyed anything that might be used to feed or supply the rebel army; terrorized the civilian population; freed more than 25,000 slaves; and shot the bloodhounds that had been used to hunt them down.

Sherman and his men were shocked to see that many of the rebels they killed in their one serious skirmish were boys (some as young as 14) and old men: a sign of the Confederacy's desperation.

Coming upon Union soldiers who had escaped from Andersonville, a Southern prisoner-of-war camp, they were stunned and infuriated at the sick and emaciated appearance of their comrades.

On December 23, Sherman wired the president that he had a Christmas present for him: the vital Confederate port of Savannah, Georgia.

Deeply gratified and relieved by the news

from Gen. Sherman, Abraham Lincoln continued to face the grave, daily responsibilities of his wartime presidency.

Always an early riser, he was invariably awake by six. He would read, write letters, and work on speeches before taking a walk and eating breakfast. He was an indifferent and light eater: An egg and coffee would do for breakfast, lunch might be an apple and a glass of milk, and dinner a chicken leg and water. During the course of the day, he met with Cabinet members, congressmen, military men, and assorted politicians and civilians who always wanted something.

One of his least favorite responsibilities was reviewing the cases of soldiers who had deserted or committed other serious offenses. There were, eventually, 250,000 deserters in the Union army. He tried to find a way to pardon anyone who was to be executed for his actions.

*"No man was yet improved by shooting him."*

*"There are already too many weeping widows in the United States, for God's sake, do not ask me to add to the number."*

Fridays were execution day, and he could hear the shots through the open window in his office.

He worked almost every night, either attending formal White House functions; going over papers; meeting with still more people; or walking across the lawn to the War Department's telegraph office. Most times, he couldn't wait until the messages were brought to him. He would stand behind the clerks and anxiously watch while they decoded the reports coming in from the numerous battles taking place across the country. There were 6.5 million coded telegrams sent over the course of the war.

At night, the operators left the telegrams in a pile for him, with the latest one on top. Sometimes, he stayed there all night.

He had few diversions to relieve him from his incomprehensibly awful burden. Most afternoons he took a carriage ride with Secy. of State Seward, friends, political associates, or Tad or Mary.

Mary had finally stopped wearing mourning and allowed some social activities at the White House. But it was clear that she would never fully recover from Willie's death and seemed more difficult with each passing day. Lincoln did not know that Mary had gone deep into debt because of her excessive clothing and jewelry purchases, or that she had asked members of his Cabinet to help her financially, further adding to her state of constant distress.

Their relationship was another casualty of the war.

Sometimes, they went to plays and sometimes, he liked to go alone. Theater managers allowed him to quietly enter through the stage door and slip into a box where he was hidden by drapes. There, far from the people who constantly hounded him, he could get his mind off the war and be distracted for a couple of hours by the comedies, dramas, and especially the plays of Shakespeare that he so enjoyed.

Lincoln lived with the knowledge that his life was in danger from the moment he was elected. Even before the president-elect left Springfield for his journey east, he had already received poisoned fruit and threatening letters. In the days surrounding his inauguration, numerous plots came to light.

In the early years of his first term, the president enjoyed walking alone through the streets of Washington late at night or in the early-morning hours. Secy. of War Stanton, who was particularly concerned about Lincoln's safety, had a small group of soldiers accompany him when he left the White House grounds. On Stanton's orders, they followed even when Lincoln walked across the lawn to the War Deptartment's telegraph office. There were soldiers stationed in the White House basement and hidden in the bushes outside. Stanton also insisted that a cavalry unit accompany the president and Mrs. Lincoln during their carriage rides. Lincoln invariably complained about the disturbing noise their spurs and sabers made.

Lincoln cooperated reluctantly. Despite the danger he knew was out there somewhere, the president believed that these measures were inappropriate.

*"It would never do for a president to have a guard with drawn sabers at his door, as if he fancied he were, or were trying to be, an emperor."*

*"Why put up bars when the fence is down all around . . . in a country like ours . . . assassination is always possible, and it will come if they are determined upon it."*

These security measures served as a constant reminder of that threat, and Lincoln refused to live in a state of fear.

In August 1862, while Lincoln was riding his horse, rifle shots knocked his hat off—probably hunters with bad aim, he joked. Now, with his reelection and the war going badly for the South, the threats on his life only increased. He filed the letters he received in an envelope marked "assassination." The very night of his reelection, his friend and self-assigned bodyguard, Ward Lamon, slept on the floor outside his door wrapped in a blanket. Lamon left in the morning before the president awoke.

Although security had been increased over

February 27, 1860          November 8, 1863

the years, it was still, at Lincoln's insistence, minimal.

———————————

As the war that was to last three months ended its third horrific year, Abraham Lincoln looked worn and unwell. He had always silently endured pain, but now the damage showed. The incessant pressure, the endless problems, the daily death count, and the legions of wounded—all of it was taking a terrible toll on him.

His once kind and expressive face had frozen permanently into a grim, ghostly look. At times, it seemed as if he were not quite there. The gray eyes that had once sparkled while he told one of his unique stories or made a telling point with a seemingly irrelevant aside were now somber and silent. Black rings encircled them and they had sunken back into his skull, as if recoiling from the horror of all they had seen.

The half-moon lines that had formed around his mouth when he was a young man (not all that many years ago) had now etched themselves deep into his too-pale skin; perhaps marking the deaths of the 620,000 boys who were to die in the war.

He had become withered, weighted down, and weakened by the unrelenting sadness and sorrow that surrounded him every moment of every day. As if the elected representative of the people had to also represent their pain and suffering.

He had grown old before his time.

Most nights he couldn't sleep. He would pace up and down, hands clasped behind his back, bent over, lost deep, deep in thought. He knew that the unprecedented and inhuman task that destiny had so clearly marked him for was far from finished.

He steeled himself to face each torturous day.

He must not waver. Not now. He willed himself to go on.

February 9, 1864

February 5, 1865

# 1865

## 13TH AMENDMENT
## SECOND INAUGURATION
## RICHMOND · APPOMATTOX

By January 1865, President Lincoln was taking time from the pressing problems of the present to look to the future to a time when the Civil War would be over and the painful process of reconstructing the country could begin.

The future of the Emancipation Proclamation and the American slaves particularly concerned him. Since it was an act by a president using his wartime powers, it might not hold up in the courts of postwar America. Lincoln wanted a permanent solution to the problem of slavery: an amendment to the Constitution of the United States.

His proposed Thirteenth Amendment, abolishing slavery forever, had been approved in the Senate in April 1864, but not in the House of Representatives. Since his reelection and its implied support of his policies, he had worked hard to get members of the House to approve the measure when it was resubmitted to them. His efforts were successful.

On January 31, 1865, the House approved the amendment by only three votes, and it was to be submitted to the individual states for ratification.

Symbolically, the new iron dome of the capitol, with the bronze Statue of Freedom now on top, was completed in time for Lincoln's second inauguration on March 4. His address was brief, but eloquent.

*"With malice toward none; with charity for all; with firmness in the right, as God gives us to see the right, let us strive on to finish the work we are in; to bind up the nation's wounds; to care for him who shall have borne the battle, and for his widow, and his orphan—to do all which may achieve and cherish a just and a lasting peace, among ourselves, and with all nations."*

After the inauguration, the president was so sick and tired he had to stay in bed—even holding a Cabinet meeting from there. He was having awful headaches, not sleeping, and had lost weight over the past few months.

*"I am a little alarmed about myself,"* the usually stoic Lincoln confided to his good friend Joshua Speed.

———

In mid-March, General Grant invited the president to visit him at his headquarters, now just 20 miles south of Richmond. Always eager to escape the pressures of living in the White House, Lincoln accepted, and Mary and Tad accompanied him.

When they first arrived, the president was scheduled to review the troops. He rode ahead to the parade grounds on horseback, while Mary and Mrs. Grant followed in an army ambulance carriage. Their jolting ride over the bumpy roads and Mary's anxiety that, due to their slow progress, they were going to be late, precipitated one of her migraines. Mary took out her frustrations on the driver and Julia Grant, and at one point, attempted to walk there.

Mary was indeed late and the president was already reviewing the troops, the commanding general's wife riding alongside him. Mary became agitated, seeing another woman in her place and fearing that people might think that she, not Mary, was the president's wife. She began screaming insults at the general's bewildered wife, bringing her to tears. Lincoln and Julia Grant tried to calm her down, but she verbally attacked them as well.

At a dinner that night, hosted by the president, Mary publicly accused him of flirting with the woman and demanded that he remove the general from command. She continued with this tirade throughout the evening.

Over the next few days, she refused to leave her room and then, leaving Tad with his father, returned alone to Washington.

Lincoln was able to see his oldest son, who was now on Grant's staff. Robert had, after failing Harvard's entrance exam, attended exclusive Phillips Exeter Academy, and then Harvard. He was accused by the president's critics of being a coward because he hadn't enlisted. The subject had long been a point of contention between his parents. His mother, who had already lost two sons, was adamantly opposed to Robert's entering the army. His father was torn: How could he send his own son to go to school while he sent thousands of other boys to their deaths?

Robert graduated in 1864, and his mother relented. He was made a captain on Grant's staff. Grant, although never asked directly by the president or his wife, saw to it that Robert was never in any real danger.

The president met with Gens. Grant and Sherman and discussed the end of the war. The situation in the South was so desperate that the Confederate government had, that same month, decided to enlist slaves as soldiers.

Sherman had come from North Carolina and had already completed his invasion of South Carolina, the first state to secede from the Union. His men were even harsher

*April 1865: Richmond, Virginia, lay in ruins after a fire set by evacuating Confederate forces.*

there than in Atlanta or during their march across Georgia to the sea.

Lincoln made it clear that he wanted true reconciliation with the people of the South.

"*. . . Get the deluded men of the rebel armies disarmed and back to their homes. . . . Let them all go, officers and all, I want submission and no more bloodshed. . . . I want no one punished; treat them liberally all around. We want those people to return to their allegiance to the union and submit to the laws.*"

On April 2, while the president was still at Grant's headquarters, Union forces captured Petersburg after a nine-month siege. Richmond was next.

Jefferson Davis was attending church when a messenger came down the aisle and handed him Gen. Lee's warning that Richmond had to be evacuated immediately. Davis and his Cabinet left the city.

Union troops entered Richmond, carefully avoiding the land mines purposely left by the retreating rebels. The rebels had also set fire to the warehouses and bridges, and the fire spread, eventually exploding the huge Confederate arsenal. An hour after they first entered the city, the rebel flag that was flying above the state capital was taken down and replaced by the Stars and Stripes.

When Lincoln was informed that Richmond was in Union hands, he said:

"*Thank God I have lived to see this! It seems to me I have been dreaming a horrid dream for four years, and now the nightmare is gone. I want to see Richmond!*"

On April 4, accompanied by Tad and guarded only by a small contingent of sailors, Lincoln arrived in what had been the capital of the Confederate States of America. He and his son rode and walked the two miles through the streets, which were littered with rubble from the destroyed and burned-out buildings.

They were surrounded by now-emancipated slaves: some weeping, others trying to touch him, all not believing that the man who had given them their freedom was there, right before their eyes.

The white residents of Richmond who remained stayed in their houses and peered out from behind curtained windows.

———————

When the president arrived back in Washington on April 9, Secy. of War Stanton handed him a telegram from Gen. Grant stating that Gen. Lee had surrendered his army that morning.

Lee's 30,000 soldiers, diminished by death and desertion, were worn and hungry. Some were barefoot, and others had no weapons and even those who did were low on ammunition. There was no hope of reinforcement or resupply. Grant's 125,000 well-fed and fully supplied men were pressing in on all sides.

President Jefferson Davis pledged that the South would fight on; they would have to be annihilated before they ceased.

No one wanted to surrender less than Lee. He had only recently told his men that it was their duty to fight to the last man. And he had considered doing just that.

How many times in the past four years had he been victorious against great odds? Holding off McClellan; at Fredericksburg and Chancellorsville; and against Grant in the Wilderness, Spotsylvania, and Cold Harbor.

Even though his men were exhausted and worse, he knew that if he called upon them again they would respond as valiantly as they had in the past.

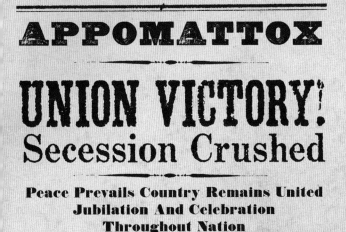

# APPOMATTOX

# UNION VICTORY!
## Secession Crushed

**Peace Prevails Country Remains United
Jubilation And Celebration
Throughout Nation**

He could disband his army and order his men to disappear into the southern landscape to live in the forests and swamps, the hills, mountains, and river valleys. From there, they could, with the willing support of the population, carry on an endless, guerrilla war, using terrorist tactics against the North. Such a war could go on for years, perhaps eventually persuading the North to allow the South its independence.

If he did surrender, what would happen to his men? Would they be taken prisoner? Put in prisoner of war camps? Paraded throughout the streets of Washington? Would he himself be executed for treason?

As he had done so often in the past, Robert E. Lee controlled his emotions, strong and deep as they were. This was a time for reason, not reaction, for reconciliation, not resistance. It was time to rebuild and reunite the country that only a few short years ago had been one and must be again.

It was time to surrender.

Courageously ignoring Davis's pledge to fight on indefinitely, Lee responded diplomatically to a note from Grant. Further cautious and courteous notes were exchanged, and a meeting was arranged.

Wearing his gray full-dress uniform, red silk sash across his waist, jeweled ceremonial sword at his side (borrowed—he never carried a weapon of any kind), 58-year-old Robert E. Lee rode out to meet his 42-year-old adversary, Ulysses S. Grant. They met at a brick house with a covered porch in the little village of Appomattox Court House, Virginia.

Grant, dressed as usual in his rumpled field uniform and mud-splattered pants and boots, arrived half an hour later, apologizing for not having had time to change.

Sitting at separate tables, they discussed Grant's generous terms—terms that reflected the president's heartfelt desire to achieve a true, lasting reconciliation and the two opposing generals' agreement with that goal.

Grant said that Lee's men would be paroled after laying down their weapons. The two men agreed that they could keep their sidearms and their horses and mules, which they would need for farming when they returned to their homes.

Lee told Grant that his men were starving along with the Union prisoners they had. Grant promised that rations for 25,000 men would be sent immediately.

Rising from the tables, they shook hands and Lee walked outside. Union officers on the porch (including Capt. Robert Lincoln) saluted the general. Before riding off on his gray stallion, Traveler, Lee lifted his hat to Grant, who had come out onto the porch and returned the gesture.

Grant allowed no celebration by his men.

Even though the Confederate States' government was still at large, 175,000 Southern soldiers were still in the field with various other armies, and there were formalities to be dispensed with, the surrender of Gen. Robert E. Lee's Army of Northern Virginia meant that the Civil War was over.

Five days later, Abraham Lincoln became the first president ever assassinated.

# C·H·R·O·N·O·L·O·G·Y

| 1806 | Thomas Lincoln marries Nancy Hanks |
|------|-------------------------------------|
| 1809 | Abraham Lincoln born, Kentucky (Feb 12) |
| 1816 | Family moves to Indiana (Dec) |
| 1818 | Mother dies (Oct) |
| 1819 | Father marries Sarah Bush Johnston (Dec) |
| 1820 | Missouri Compromise |
| 1828 | Older sister dies (Jan) |
| 1830 | Family moves to Illinois (Mar) |
| 1831 | Settles in New Salem, Illinois (July) |
| 1832 | Enlists in militia (April)<br>Loses election to State Legislature (Aug)<br>Buys general store (Aug) |
| 1833 | Appointed postmaster (May)<br>Appointed deputy Surveyor |
| 1834 | Elected to Illinois House of Representatives (Aug) |
| 1836 | Reelected to Illinois House of Representatives (Aug)<br>Receives law license (Sept) |
| 1837 | Moves to Springfield, Illinois (April)<br>Enters law practice with John Stuart |
| 1838 | Reelected to Illinois House of Representatives (Aug) |
| 1840 | Reelected to Illinois House of Representatives (Aug) |
| 1841 | Enters law practice with Stephen Logan (April) |
| 1842 | Marries Mary Todd (Nov) |
| 1843 | Robert Todd Lincoln born (Aug) |
| 1844 | Enters law practice with William Herndon (Dec) |
| 1846 | Edward "Eddie" Baker Lincoln born (Mar)<br>Elected to U.S. House of Representatives (Aug) |

| 1847 | Arrives in Washington |
|------|------------------------|
| 1849 | Congressional term ends, returns to Springfield (Mar) |
| 1850 | Eddie dies (Feb)<br>William Wallace "Willie" Lincoln born (Dec) |
| 1853 | Thomas "Tad" Lincoln born (April) |
| 1854 | Kansas/Nebraska Act (May)<br>Elected to Illinois State Legislature (Nov) |
| 1855 | Loses election for U.S. Senate (Feb) |
| 1856 | Joins Republican Party (Feb)<br>Sen. Sumner attacked (May) |
| 1857 | *Dred Scott* decision (Mar) |
| 1858 | Lincoln/Douglas Debates (Aug–Oct)<br>Loses election for U.S. Senate (Nov) |
| 1859 | John Brown's raid on Harper's Ferry (Oct) |
| 1860 | Speech at Cooper Union (Feb)<br>Nominated to run for President of the United States (May)<br>Elected President of the United States (Nov)<br>South Carolina secedes (Dec) |
| 1861 | Mississippi, Florida, Alabama, Georgia, and Louisiana secede (Jan)<br>Texas secedes (Feb)<br>Leaves Springfield for Washington (Feb)<br>Jefferson Davis inaugurated President of Confederate States of America (Feb)<br>Inaugurated sixteenth President of United States (Mar)<br>Fort Sumter surrenders (April)<br>Calls for 75,000 volunteers (April)<br>Robert E. Lee refuses command of Union army, returns to Virginia (April)<br>Sixth Massachusetts regiment attacked in Baltimore (April)<br>Arkansas, North Carolina, and Virginia secede (May)<br>Tennessee secedes (June)<br>Richmond becomes capital of Confederate States of America (May) |

First Battle of Bull Run (July)

George McClellan becomes commander of
    Military Division of the Potomac (July)

**1862**  Willie dies (Feb)

Ulysses S. Grant captures Forts Henry and
    Donelson (Feb)

McClellan begins Peninsula Campaign
    (April)

Battle of Shiloh (April)

Lee becomes commander of Army of
    Northern Virginia (June)

Seven Days Battle (June/July)

Emancipation Proclamation presented to
    Cabinet (July)

Second Battle of Bull Run (Aug)

Battle of Antietam (Sept)

Preliminary Emancipation Proclamation
    issued (Sept)

Battle of Fredericksburg (Dec)

**1863**  Issues Emancipation Proclamation (Jan)

Battle of Chancellorsville/Thomas
    "Stonewall" Jackson killed (May)

Battle of Gettysburg (July)

Grant captures Vicksburg (July)

New York Draft Riots (July)

Fifty-fourth Massachussets regiment
    assaults Fort Wagner (July)

Gettysburg Address (Nov)

**1864**  Grant becomes Gen. in Chief of U.S. Army
    (March)

William Tecumseh Sherman becomes
    commander  of U.S. Army in West
    (March)

Grant's Virginia offensive begins (May)

Battle of the Wilderness (May)

Battle of Spotsylvania (May)

Battle of Cold Harbor (May/June)

Renominated to run for presidency (June)

Sherman occupies Atlanta (Sept)

Reelected President of the United States
    (Nov)

Sherman begins March to the Sea (Nov)

Sherman occupies Savannah (Dec)

**1865**  Congress passes Thirteenth Amendment
    (Jan)

Robert E. Lee becomes Gen. in Chief of
    Confederate Army (Feb)

Second inauguration (March)

Confederates withdraw from Petersburg,
    Virginia (April)

Federal troops enter Richmond (April)

Visits Richmond (April)

Lee surrenders to Grant (April 9)

Abraham Lincoln shot at Ford's Theater
    (April 14)

Abraham Lincoln Dies (April 15, 7:22 AM)

Buried in Springfield (May)

# ★·I·N·D·E·X·★

# PICTURE CREDITS

★ ★ ★ ★ ★

## Bibliography Notice

An extensive bibliography of books and other media about Abraham Lincoln, the assassination, Mary Lincoln, the Civil War, and related topics is available to view and download at mackids.com.

# O CAPTAIN! MY CAPTAIN!

### DEDICATED TO THE

## HON. ABRM. LINCOLN

★ ★ ★ ★

## WORDS BY WALT WHITMAN, 1865

O Captain! my Captain! our fearful trip is done,
The ship has weather'd every rack, the prize we sought is won,
The port is near, the bells I hear, the people all exulting,
While follow eyes the steady keel, the vessel grim and daring.
        But O heart! heart! heart!
          O the bleeding drops of red,
            Where on the deck my Captain lies,
            Fallen cold and dead.

O Captain! my Captain! rise up and hear the bells;
Rise up—for you the flag is flung—for you the bugle trills,
For you bouquets and ribbon'd wreaths—for you the shores a-crowding.
For you they call, the swaying mass, their eager faces turning.
        Here Captain! dear father!
          This arm beneath your head!
            It is some dream that on the deck,
            You've fallen cold and dead.

My Captain does not answer, his lips are pale and still
My father does not feel my arm, he has no pulse nor will,
The ship is anchor'd safe and sound, its voyage closed and done,
From fearful trip the victor ship comes in with object won;
        Exult O shores, and ring O bells!
        But I with mournful tread,
          Walk the deck my Captain lies,
          Fallen cold and dead.

# BARRY DENENBERG

is the author of the critically acclaimed *Voices from Vietnam*, as well as biographies of Charles Lindbergh, Anne Frank, Nelson Mandela, and Elvis Presley. Before writing history books for young readers, he held various management positions at publishing houses and national book retailers, and ghostwrote reviews for NPR. Today, he continues to write children's books, including the upcoming *Titanic Sinks!* and operates the manuscript company BD/A, which he founded. Barry is married to publisher Jean Feiwel. They have a daughter, Emma, who attends New York University, and a rescued chocolate Newfoundland named Holden. Visit him online at barrydenenberg.com.

# CHRISTOPHER BING

won a 2001 Caldecott Honor Award for *Casey at the Bat*, the classic 1888 poem. He also illustrated *The Midnight Ride of Paul Revere*, which was called "an impressive volume" (*Publishers Weekly*) and "a remarkable visual interpretation of Longfellow's classic poem" (*Booklist*). Mr. Bing lives in Massachusetts with his wife Wendy and their three children. Visit him on the Web at christopherbing.com.

SQUARE
FISH
AN IMPRINT OF MACMILLAN

LINCOLN SHOT. TEXT COPYRIGHT © 2008 BY BARRY DENENBERG. ILLUSTRATIONS COPYRIGHT © 2008 BY CHRISTOPHER BING. ALL RIGHTS RESERVED. PRINTED IN CHINA BY RR DONNELLEY ASIA PRINTIN SOLUTIONS LTD., DONGGUAN CITY, GUANGDONG PROVINCE. FOR INFORMATION, ADDRESS SQUARE FISH, 175 FIFTH AVENUE, NEW YORK, NY 10010.

LIBRARY OF CONGRESS CATALOGING-IN-PUBLICATION DATA

DENENBERG, BARRY. LINCOLN SHOT! : A PRESIDENT'S LIFE REMEMBERED / BY BARRY DENENBERG ; ILLUSTRATIONS BY CHRISTOPHER BING.    P. CM.
ISBN 978-0-312-60442-4
[1.  LINCOLN, ABRAHAM, 1809–1865—JUVENILE LITERATURE. 2.  PRESIDENTS—UNITED STATES—BIOGRAPHY—JUVENILE LITERATURE. 3.  LINCOLN, ABRAHAM, 1809–1865—ASSASSINATION—JUVENILE LITERATURE.]  I. TITLE.
E457.905.D46 2008    973.7092—DC22    [B]    2007048851

ORIGINALLY PUBLISHED IN THE UNITED STATES BY FEIWEL AND FRIENDS

FIRST SQUARE FISH EDITION: DECEMBER 2011

SQUARE FISH LOGO DESIGNED BY FILOMENA TUOSTO
BOOK DESIGN BY RICH DEAS AND BARBARA GRZESLO

MACKIDS.COM

10 9 8 7 6 5 4

★★★★★★★★★
SQUARE FISH
★★★★★★★★★

FEIWEL AND FRIENDS

PUBLISHERS OF FINE QUALITY BOOKS SINCE 2006

*Researched, written, illustrated, and designed*
by **The National News** *staff:*

*Chief Writer* **Barry Denenberg**
*Artist* **Christopher Bing**  *Creative Director* **Rich Deas**
*Editor* **Kate Waters, Jessica Tedder**
*Staff* **Martin Baldessari, Dave Barrett, Kathleen Breitenfeld, Susan Doran, Barbara Grzeslo, Bradley Rife, Kaitlin Severini, Holly West**
*Publisher* **Jean Feiwel**